THE
"QUESTIONED STOCK"
MANUAL

THE "QUESTIONED STOCK" MANUAL

A GUIDE TO DETERMINING THE
TRUE WORTH OF
OLD AND COLLECTIBLE SECURITIES

ALBERT F. GARGIULO
with
Rocco Carlucci

McGRAW-HILL BOOK COMPANY

New York ■ St. Louis ■ San Francisco ■ Auckland
Bogotá ■ Düsseldorf ■ Johannesburg ■ London ■ Madrid ■ Mexico
Montreal ■ New Delhi ■ Panama ■ Paris ■ São Paulo
Singapore ■ Sydney ■ Tokyo ■ Toronto

Library of Congress Cataloging in Publication Data

Gargiulo, Albert F
The "questioned stock" manual.

Includes index.
1. Securities, Obsolete—United States.
I. Carlucci, Rocco, joint author. II. Title.
HG4927.G37   332.6'32   78-27451
ISBN 0-07-022865-5

1234567890   MUBP   7865432109

The editor for this book was W. Hodson Mogan,
the designer was William Frost, and the production supervisor was
Sally Fliess. It was set in Electra by Monotype Composition Company, Inc.

Printed by The Murray Printing Company and bound by The Book Press.

to Beth Ann and Kathleen
for their love and understanding
and to the fond memory
of Anthony Carlucci

CONTENTS

PREFACE   xi

CHAPTER ONE

STOCK TRADING AND THE ORIGINS OF
"QUESTIONED STOCK"   1

    History of Stock and Stock Trading ▪ The Name Game:
    Mergers and Acquisitions

CHAPTER TWO

SUCCESS STORIES   21

Sleuth ▪ Tracer ▪ The Doctor's Library ▪ The Engineer's Windfall ▪ The Nudist's Certificate ▪ The Baker's Estate ▪ The Lucky Schoolteacher ▪ The Woman Who Changed Her Mind ▪ Dig Deep

CHAPTER THREE

THE INVESTIGATION: I   33

Recommended Procedure ▪ Starting Point: The Certificate Itself ▪ Sources of Further Information ▪ The Secretary of State ▪ The Securities and Exchange Commission ▪ The Transfer Agent and Registrar ▪ The National Association of Securities Dealers ▪ Contacting the Company and Its Officers Directly

CHAPTER FOUR

THE INVESTIGATION: II   63

R. M. Smythe & Company, Inc. ▪ The *Directory of Obsolete Securities* ▪ The *National Monthly Stock Summary* ▪ An Example: Resdel Industries ▪ The News Media ▪ Other Sources

CHAPTER FIVE

SAVE THAT PRETTY WALLPAPER:
Stock Certificates As "Collectibles"   95

The Mining Securities

CHAPTER SIX

DETECTION AND RECOGNITION OF FRAUDULENT SECURITIES   103

Security Printing ▪ Stringent Requirements for Valuable Documents ▪ Aids in Detecting Counterfeits ▪ Ten Quick Checks for Genuineness

APPENDIX: Sixty Years of Corporate Ups, Downs, and Outs
(1917–1977)   119

GLOSSARY   177

INDEX   187

PREFACE

The year is 2080. The world has grown, prospered, changed. It has survived. New technologies and advances have made life-styles quite different from those of a hundred years ago. The planets have been visited; the depths of the seas have been explored. For the moment at least, however precariously, the world is at peace.

In the new world of 100 years hence, everything is computerized. Normal everyday chores can now be effortlessly accomplished by the push of a button. Vast memory banks store as much information on a chip the size of a pinhead as once filled a dozen file cabinets. Virtually all the world's records can now instantaneously and individually appear on a video screen at the user's command.

A young man living in the great northeastern megalopolis of the United States has just received his share of his grandfather's estate. As he opens the large brown envelope he finds several elaborately engraved documents. Although such items have not been used for the past fifty-odd years, he knows that they are stock certificates. He counts them: five 100-share certificates. The name of the company, however, seems unfamiliar, obscure. Instinctively, he turns on his video screen and tunes in to the day's news. He punches in the code for the financial report. Anticipation. He quickly scans the list of companies, skipping over the first six letters of the alphabet. Finally he gets the G's and searches for a company called General Motors. Not there. Surely there's some mistake. His grandfather was a wise and successful businessman. He would never have invested in some fly-by-night company, let alone leave worthless paper to his favorite grandson. It must be there. He punches in another code and makes a call. "General Motors?" the stockbroker responds. "I remember hearing of it some years back. I don't know the ticker symbol, nor do I see it on my listings. I'll check with my central information memory bank and get back to you." *Maybe my grandfather did take a flyer once in a while,* muses the puzzled young man. *If nothing else, I'll paper my walls.*

In this fast-moving and ever-changing world of ours, the scenario you've just read may not be as preposterous as it may seem. It was just sixty years ago that Marconi Wireless Telegraph Company of America was a very pop-

ular and well-known firm. However, you will not find it in
the financial section of today's newspapers, nor will it
"cross the tape" on the floor of any exchange. Are its shares
worthless? Hardly. To this day Marconi shares are still convertible into shares of RCA Corporation, which itself was
formerly known as the Radio Corporation of America.

Every year hundreds of companies change their
names, are merged into or are acquired by other companies, or liquidate their businesses, leaving behind an
enormous amount of obsolete securities. These are the
"questioned stocks," the subject of this book; they may be
either bought or inherited, and they are often assumed
worthless since, for one reason or another, their holders
are unable to find a price quote or obtain any other information about them.

Some of these stocks are indeed worthless, the last
remains of a once mighty enterprise forced into oblivion
because of its inability to change with the times, or perhaps the only thing left of a dreamer's folly.

However, in many instances (as is the case with the
Marconi example) these securities still have value—occasionally a fortune.

The theme of this book is the tracing of securities that
have become obsolete. The procedures set forth will supply
the user with the information necessary to conduct a
thorough, decisive, and conclusive investigation of those
securities which have become unfamiliar to most. The
reader should keep in mind that "obsolete" is not in all
cases tantamount to "defunct."

Fortunes have been discovered in securities that were intended to be part of a very colorful and intriguing wall décor; others remain just that.

A beep. Another one. The young man answers. "Good news," the stockbroker announces. "I've discovered that about thirty years ago General Motors changed its name to Interplanetary Starship Corporation. Your shares are still convertible. They are worth a good deal of money."

Full of gratitude, the young man hangs up. He smiles. "Sly old fox, my grandfather," he says aloud.

CHAPTER ONE

STOCK TRADING AND THE ORIGINS OF "QUESTIONED STOCK"

Are there really immense fortunes waiting "out there" to be claimed by the lucky owners of old stock certificates gathering dust in some forgotten trunk in an attic corner or adorning a wall as chic but seemingly worthless decorative paper? If so, how can this come about, and how can these potential windfalls be realized?

The present chapter will begin to address these questions. A brief history of stock and stock trading is included, along with a discussion of one of the most common reasons why stocks slip into obscurity, that is, alteration or complete change of a company's name—for example, through mergers and acquisitions.

Yes, unclaimed fortunes do exist. It was estimated in the mid-1930s by O. P. Schwarzschild, then president of R. M. Smythe & Company, specialists in evaluation of obscure and unusual securities, that there were approximately $300 million worth of obsolete securities in the hands of the public. Among the reasons for this were the stock market crash of 1929 and the great Depression that followed; the infancy of the Securities and Exchange Commission; the nonexistence of various other regulatory agencies; and much less stringent requirements for financial reporting by public companies.

Since many of these excesses have been corrected, one might assume that the value of obsolete securities in the hands of the public today would be considerably less, but this does not seem to be the case. There is a great deal more corporate activity nowadays, including mergers, acquisitions, liquidations, spinoffs, and the like, and this will continue.

A conservative estimate of today's public holdings of "questioned stocks" runs into the billions of dollars! In addition, many of these securities have been accumulating dividends over the years—amounts held in escrow waiting to be claimed by the rightful owners. In some cases, the accumulated dividends have even been more than the value of the underlying security!

In order to explain how this has happened—realizing, of course, that some impatient readers will prefer to skip to the following chapters and begin tracing their obsolete securities at once—we now provide some useful historical background, aimed especially at those who know little about the stock market.

HISTORY OF STOCK AND STOCK TRADING

Relative to the history of the world, it was not so long ago that people had to carry "hard" commodities (livestock, bricks, nails, crops, cloth, and the like) in order to trade for other commodities they needed for survival. This, of course, was the barter system—trading one good or service for another needed good or service.

As civilizations and governments developed, a medium of exchange called "money" was introduced. At first this, too, was "hard" money: gold, silver, bronze, copper. And again the system was cumbersome. Another aspect of this era was the primitive nature of record keeping. Property divisions, for example, were marked on trees or rocks.

The progressive technologies of more modern times have shown that greater efficiency and convenience can be achieved by using surrogate means of expressing rights, powers, and possessions. Today, our answer to a carved tablet or heavy coin is the paper document.

For all intents and purposes, these documents are accepted as having a value equivalent to that of their underlying intrinsic worth. These documents take many forms: deeds to real property, bank notes, currency, corporate or municipal bonds, stamps, letters of credit, stock certificates and other securities, commercial paper, and drafts.

One of the items mentioned, the stock certificate, traces its beginnings to some 500 years before the Continental Congress was established. It is widely accepted that in June 1288 one Peter Elofsson, a bishop, purchased approximately a 12 percent interest in a Swedish copper mine. The company—Stora Kopparbergs Bergslags Aktiebolag—is still actively extracting minerals from the mine today and is generally believed to be the world's oldest corporation.

Some 350 years later, in the early 1620s, the Dike Corporation (Lekdyk Bovendams of Holland) issued stock to help finance the construction of a dike along the lowland area of the Lek River. This document still draws an annual dividend and is now owned by the New York Stock Exchange.

In today's complex financial structure, millions of shares of various securities change hands every business day. The advanced technology of our era facilitates these transfers with a speed and accuracy unprecedented in the history of stock trading. However, the idea of a securities marketplace is by no means a new phenomenon.

The first proposal for a joint stock bank in Athens occurred during the reign of Xenophon and, had it been adopted, would have led to the formation of a stock exchange. In 1344, in the state of Florence, and again in 1407, in the republic of Genoa, huge amounts of debt were converted into the capital of a bank. Consequently, the creditors became stockholders of the newly formed institution, and their "shares"—being transferable—were actively traded.

In England, the office of Royal Exchanger was established in several cities for the purpose of exchanging money —gold for silver, foreign for English. These establishments were dubbed "exchanges," and merchants met regularly for the intended purpose. In time, these merchants began trading and speculating in other commodities such as tobacco, cotton, and livestock, and, ultimately, shares of stock. The first officially designated "Stock Exchange" was established in New Jonathan's Coffee House in London in July 1773.

The origin of the word "stock" is the Anglo-Saxon *stocc*, literally "a piece of wood." Since this was the primary source of fuel in those days, it had to be gathered and stored for cooking and heat. Thus, anything accumulated or stockpiled was referred to as *stock*.

In England until 1785 borrower and lender kept track of their financial dealings by cutting notches in a piece of wood known as a *tally*. The slip of wood was split in half, with the debtor's and creditor's names and transaction dates on each side. One was referred to as the *stock* and the other the *counterstock* (an exact match of the two split halves prevented fraud). These tallies were transferable and traded, very much like our present-day stock certificates. It was not until many years later that William IV ordered all tallies in the government's possession destroyed by fire. What was not anticipated, however, was that during the process a freak accident occurred that burned down both Houses of Parliament.

The term "to trade" developed from the old company-store concept. In England, workers received their wages in the form of a token intrinsically equivalent to 24 grains of silver, redeemable only by their employer for food, clothing, shelter, and the like. The workers would "trade" (i.e., pledge or pawn) these tokens for goods, and hence the concept was established.*

Securities trading in America originated, as did many of our other institutions, during the War for Independence. The story that follows is a fascinating account of the forming of the world's richest and most sophisticated securities marketplace:

> Wall Street once was the political capital of the United States just as it is the financial center of the world today. Here the New York State Chamber of Commerce, established April 5, 1768, pressed the fight on the Stamp Act and the tax on tea. Here Washington took the first Presidential oath of office, here the first Congress gathered, its executive departments were organized, and the immortal Bill of Rights was adopted.
>
> It was there that the 1789–90 Congress authorized an issue of $80 million in stock to help pay for the costs of the Revolutionary War. There was a scattered market for this government stock as well as for the shares of banks and insurance companies then springing up. Trading was carried on in various coffee houses, auction rooms, and offices, but it was mostly unorganized and people were reluctant to invest because they had no assurance they could sell their securities when they wanted to do so.
>
> On May 17, 1792, a group of merchants and auctioneers met to do something about this situation. They decided to meet daily at regular hours to buy and sell securities under

---

* The authors are grateful to the American Bank Note Company for allowing the use of their research data and facilities.

an old buttonwood tree on Wall Street only a few blocks from the present site of the Stock Exchange.

These twenty-four men were the original members of the Exchange. They handled the public's buy and sell orders in the new government stock, as well as in shares of insurance companies, Alexander Hamilton's First United States Bank, the Bank of North America, and the Bank of New York.

In 1793, the Tontine Coffee House was completed at the northwest corner of Wall and William Streets and the brokers moved indoors.

Private financial activity was checked for a time by the War of 1812, but peace brought the formation of new enterprises. New York State bonds, issued to pay for the Erie Canal, joined the issues traded on the new exchange. Private businesses also expanded. The cotton industry, able to boast only a few mills in 1804, was operating half a million spindles by 1815. The tempo of business quickened as the country headed into a post-war boom.

By 1827, the stocks of twelve banks and nineteen marine and fire insurance companies, the Delaware & Hudson Canal Co., the Merchants' Exchange, and the New York Gas Light Company—the nation's first public utility—also were traded on the Exchange.

Ten years later the list included eight railroad securities. As other new enterprises developed, their securities, too, came to the Exchange, and trading activity gradually increased. The builders of our country's pioneer companies had discovered that investors placed marketability high among the requirements for a desirable investment. It became apparent, soon after the turn of the century, that the Tontine Coffee House was too small to accommodate the volume of trading in securities, and the stock brokers moved to a meeting room in what is now 40 Wall Street. Greater activity brought the need for a more formal organization than that created by the 1792 agreement. On March 8, 1817, the first formal constitution of the New York Stock and Exchange Board, as it was then known, was adopted.

The constitution provided, among other things, that the president was to call out the names of stocks, fix commissicns, and set fines—six to twenty-five cents—for violation of procedure or non-attendance at sessions "unless when sick or out of the city."

Each trading session consisted of a morning call at 11:30 of all stocks on the list. As the name of each stock was called, the brokers made their bids and offers.

From 1817 to 1827 the Board met in various offices. After that, it moved a dozen times or so before settling, in 1863, upon the site of the present Broad Street Building, erected in 1903, which contains most of today's trading floor. The adjoining office building at the corner of Broad and Wall Streets was erected in 1922. The bond trading room and the public Exhibit Hall of Industry and Investment are housed in a newer building at 20 Broad Street.

Other historic dates are: 1863, when the name "New York Stock Exchange" was adopted; 1867, when the first stock tickers were installed; 1868, when memberships were made salable; 1871, when the call market gave way to a continuous market; 1879, when the first telephones were installed in the Exchange; 1886, the first time that a day's volume topped 1,000,000 shares; 1910, when the Exchange discontinued unlisted trading (previously an unlisted stock could be traded but the company had no responsibility to comply with Exchange standards); 1915, when the basis of quoting and trading in stocks changed from percent of par value to dollars; 1922, when the questionnaire system for periodic examination of the financial condition of member firms was inaugurated; 1933, when independent audits of financial statements were required of listed companies; and 1938, when a sweeping reorganization of the Exchange called for a paid president for the first time.[1]

THE NAME GAME: MERGERS AND ACQUISITIONS

One of the most common reasons why stocks slip into obscurity (and become seemingly obsolete and worthless) is alteration or complete change of a company's name.

"What's in a name?" asked Juliet in Shakespeare's classic. "That which we call a rose by any other name would smell as sweet." The essence of her statement, like that of countless other Shakespearean quotations, can be applied here as in so many aspects of our lives.

Some companies are involved in mergers or are acquired by other companies, thus losing their own identity. Others adopt a new, more descriptive title to express an expanded image. Still others capitalize on a valuable trademark. Activities such as these have created and will continue to create "questioned stocks."

There has been an unprecedented number of mergers and acquisitions over the past twenty years—100,000 being a conservative estimate—and the more mergers and acquisitions there are the more companies lose their identities.

In 1921, a newlywed bride received a wedding gift of 100 shares of the Chalmers Motor Corporation. With the dramatic events that took place over the years that followed,

---

[1] *Understanding the New York Stock Exchange.* Reprinted by permission of the New York Stock Exchange, Inc., 11 Wall Street, New York, NY 10005.

the shares were thought to be worthless. It was not until about ten years ago that the woman discovered that, through a series of mergers and stock splits, her old Chalmers Motor certificates were worth the equivalent of 326 shares of Chrysler Corporation.

ED GOLDFADER
PRESIDENT,
TRACERS COMPANY
OF AMERICA, INC.

Would you ever think of looking for a copper mine inside an oil field? In fact, that's exactly where you'll find one. Anaconda, a well-established corporate giant, is now part (via acquisition) of Atlantic Richfield, a leading oil company.

Anderson [Chairman of the Board, Atlantic Richfield Company] was receptive when Thomas M. Evans of Crane Company called up last March to see if he was interested in acquiring Anaconda now. Evans had tendered for 19 percent of Anaconda's shares late in 1975, with debentures valued at about $18 per share. But in February Tenneco negotiated a deal with Anaconda's management to offer $25.50 each for the remaining shares. Evans suggested to Anderson that if Arco still wanted Anaconda, it had better get moving. Days later Anderson tendered $27 per share for a 27 percent interest, thus forcing Tenneco to back away. Evans, in return for giving Anderson the right of first refusal of his 19 percent block, came away from the skirmish with a higher price for his shares.

With several months to look over the company more closely, Anderson became very much more interested in acquiring Anaconda than he had been before. Last year's $40 million loss doesn't particularly bother him. More important to him is that Anaconda is rid of its large foreign investment [in Chile] now, and that it has substantial reserves of copper, uranium, bauxite and other minerals in the U.S. plus $215 million in tax-loss carry-forwards. So on July 2 Anderson offered cash and stock worth $32 per share, or over $500 million, for the remaining 73 percent of Anaconda's shares and also lent the company $100 million.

Anaconda's book value per share is about $55.[2]

Although both of these companies are members of what are known as the "extractive" industries, the marriage is somewhat unique. Who ever thought of a giant like Anaconda falling prey to a tender offer? In most cases it is a small company that is acquired by one many times its size. Remember Sunshine Bakers (Hydrox cookies)? They are now part of American Brands. Jergens lotion? Also American Brands. How about Paramount Pictures (*The Godfather, Parts I* and *II*)? It's now a subsidiary of Gulf + Western Industries. The O. M. Scott & Sons Company (turf-builders) now belongs to International Telephone & Telegraph (ITT). These are some examples of questioned stocks which are still alive and doing very well under the guise of other names.

Year after year hundreds of companies lose their identity by either merger or acquisition. As with many other aspects of the securities industry, mergers and acquisitions are not a new phenomenon.

The most recent wave of this kind of activity was fore-

[2] "Patience Rewarded," *Forbes Magazine*, July 15, 1976. Reprinted by permission.

shadowed by three others in modern times of approximately equal magnitude: from 1868 to 1903, during the late 1920s, and again during the late 1960s. It is interesting to note that each of these three eras represented a period of rapidly rising stock market prices and an aura of general economic prosperity. All three merger waves have some characteristics in common and some that are unique. This uniqueness is most apparent in the merger wave that reached its apex in 1968. The Bureau of Economics of the Federal Trade Commission, which dates this wave as commencing in 1948, provides information to measure the magnitude of activity for those companies in the mining and manufacturing industries.

The data show that the trend toward mergers and acquisitions went continuously upward from 1948 to 1968, with very sharp rises in 1967 and 1968. Over the 1948–1968 period there were approximately 15,000 acquisitions, of which about 1,300 were of firms with assets greater than $10 million. A most startling finding was that of the 1,000 largest manufacturing and mining companies of 1950, 327 were acquired. A calculation in this study led to the conclusion that by 1968 there were about 850 fewer corporations with assets of $25 million or greater than there would have been if no mergers or acquisitions had taken place.

Some figures assembled on nonmanufacturing and nonmining acquisitions, although incomplete, are also interesting. From 1949 to 1968 some 760 retail grocery concerns, with annual sales estimated at $7.7 billion, were acquired. During 1967, 1968, and the first nine months of 1969, the 200 largest manufacturing firms acquired some

40 firms in retailing service, finance, and construction, each having assets of at least $10 million. The total value of the acquired assets during this short period was about $10 billion.

Mergers can be classified in several different ways. From a legal viewpoint, they can be divided into two categories: consolidations and acquisitions. The acquisition route, where one firm takes over another, generally by acquiring a controlling interest in its common stock, has been much more important in the recent merger wave than that of consolidation, in which a new legal entity is formed from two or more companies. A much more meaningful classification of mergers can also be made on the basis of the relation between the products and services of the acquiring and acquired firms. A merger is called *horizontal* if the product and services of the two firms compete for the same markets. A merger is said to be *vertical* if the two firms have an actual or potential supplier-customer relationship. Mergers are said to be *conglomerate* if there are neither horizontal nor vertical relationships between the merging firms. Conglomerate mergers are generally subdivided into three further categories: market extension, in which the products of the two firms are closely competitive but are sold in different geographic markets; product extension, in which the products have similarities but are not closely competitive, such as cans and bottles; and "pure," in which the products and services are virtually completely unrelated. It is worth noting that a merger of two diversified firms can have horizontal, vertical, and conglomerate aspects.

The FTC's Bureau of Economics classified 37.5 percent of the large acquisitions ($10 million or more in terms of acquired assets) as conglomerate in the 1948–1957 period. But by 1968, some 88 percent of such acquisitions were of the conglomerate type. Although product extension mergers continued to be important, the "pure" conglomerate mergers became increasingly dominant through the 1960s.

One obviously important feature of the 1960s merger wave was the "conglomerateness" of the firms after the mergers. Critical observers have taken delight in pointing out that one firm may be in meat packing and ladies underwear (Esmark, formerly Swift), another in cigars and audio-visual equipment (American Brands). Diversification is not, of course, by itself undesirable; indeed, it is a wise strategy in an era of rapidly changing markets, technologies, and needs. Many have queried whether it is possible for the management of one firm to evaluate and run an acquisition in a completely different line of work. Those engaged in building conglomerates, not unmindful of the effect of such criticism on their common stock prices, have found it necessary to try to give at least some semblance of logic to their pattern of acquisition. Thus, such disparate activities as boat building and motion picture making are grouped together as catering to the "leisure" market, while copper mining and oil drilling both become "extractive" industries.

Many of the examples set forth in the extract that follows[3] will surprise you. Some of the names will be familiar,

---

[3] © 1977, Financial Information, Inc.

others obscure, but all the examples listed, although just a fraction of those that exist, show the positive side of "questioned stocks."

What's in a name? Possibly a fortune!

Canada Dry Ginger Ale, Inc. (Del.)
>   Capital Stock no par changed to $5 par in 1933.
>   Capital Stock $5 par reclassified as Common $5 par in 1942.
>   Each share Common $5 par exchanged for (3) shares Common $1.66 2/3 par in 1946.
>   Name changed to Canada Dry Corp. 2/3/58.
>   Canada Dry Corp. merged into Simon (Norton), Inc. 7/17/68.

Decca Records, Inc. (N.Y.)
>   Each share Capital Stock $1 par exchanged for (2) shares Capital Stock 50¢ par in 1946.
>   Merged into MCA, Inc. 1/1/66.
>   Each share Capital Stock 50¢ par exchanged for $48.50 in cash.

Electrolux Corp. (Del.)
>   Common $1 par split (2) for (1) by issuance of (1) additional share 5/5/64.
>   Common $1 par split (2) for (1) by issuance of (1) additional share 5/12/66.
>   Merged into Consolidated Foods Corp. 7/1/68.
>   Each share Common $1 par exchanged for (0.32) share $4.50 Conv. Preferred Ser. A no par.

Ex-Lax Manufacturing Co. (N.Y.)

Name changed to Ex-Lax, Inc. 10/31/31.
(See Ex-Lax, Inc.)

Ex-Lax, Inc. (N.Y.)
(6% Preferred $10) 300605 30 0
(Class A Common $10) 300605 10 2
(Class B Common $10) 300605 20 1
Merged into General Cigar Co., Inc. 9/3/71.
Each share 6% Preferred $10 par exchanged for $25.80 cash.
Each share Class A Common $10 par or Class B Common $10 par exchanged for $672 cash.

Field & Stream Publishing Co.
Merged into Holt (Henry) & Co. Inc. in 1951.
Each share Common $2 par exchanged for (0.3) share 5½% Preferred $10 par, (0.5) share Common $1 par, and $7 cash.

Grace National Bank (N.Y.)
Stock dividends 12½%, 9/28/45; 33⅓%, 5/11/51; 50%, 1/30/61.
Liquidation completed.
Each share Capital Stock $100 par received initial distribution of (5) shares Marine Midland Corp. $5.50 Conv. Preferred no par 8/26/65.
Each share Capital Stock $100 par received second and final distribution of (0.765) share Marine Midland Corp. $5.50 Conv. Preferred no par 9/15/65.

Jaguar Cars Ltd. (England)

CHAPTER TWO

SUCCESS STORIES*

This chapter includes real-life examples of "stock sleuthing" on the part of several experts in the field. The stories told here should prove instructive and encouraging, whetting the reader's appetite for the next two chapters, which describe in detail methods of investigating questioned stocks.

---

* For material used in this chapter, the authors are deeply indebted to Micheline Massé, Ed Goldfader, and R. M. Smythe & Company.

SLEUTH

Dwight H. Ellis, Jr., was typical of many shareholders who are unaware of the value of their forgotten stock certificates. Either they inherited these shares or purchased them years ago and completely lost track of the companies. These stocks do not appear in financial reports and often are presumed worthless; in Mr. Ellis's case, however, as we shall see, 1000 shares in a defunct oil company turned out to be worth well in excess of $70,000.

While a Harvard student back in 1937, Mr. Ellis invested $250 with the help of his father, who at the time was a stockbroker, and purchased 1000 shares of North European Oil Corporation stock for a quarter a share. Assuming that the effects of World War II had wiped out his investment, Mr. Ellis lost track of the company, stashed the certificates in an old filing cabinet, and "was hanging on to them as a souvenir." In February of 1976, Mr. Ellis was able to determine the true status of his investment, through the services of a Montreal-based "stock sleuth" company.[1]

The president of this search firm, Micheline Massé, reconstructed for us the fate of the North European Oil Corporation.

> This company, organized in the state of Delaware in 1929, had an authorized capital stock of 4 million shares with a par value of $1.00 per share.
>
> On October 28, 1957, it was liquidated, and each com-

---

[1] Stock Market Information Service Inc., Post Office Box 120, Station "K," Montreal, Canada, H1N 3K9.

mon share was exchanged for one (1) share of North European Oil Corporation (Delaware).

In 1968 and 1969, there were stock dividends of 2 percent and 3 percent respectively.

On December 9, 1975, North European Oil Corporation was reorganized as North European Trust Company on the basis of two (2) certificates of beneficial interest in the new company for each share of stock in the old company.

The North European Trust Company is a holding company whose principal assets are in oil and gas properties, leases, and concessions located in Germany.

Since World War II, oil and gas have been reached and produced, and the company has been receiving royalties on such production.

Exchange privileges are still open to shareholders of the old corporation on the above-mentioned basis, and accrued dividends are being held by the company.

The foregoing is by no means unique. Often unknown companies, left for dead, are in fact prosperous and active under a different name. In North America alone, more than 6000 mergers take place every year; it is not hard to understand, therefore, why one can lose track of stocks which may now be valuable.

It is also interesting to note that during periods of high opulence and soaring stock market prices, the mood of the general investing public lends itself to greater degrees of speculation in the stock of relatively small and unseasoned companies. Two of these periods, the late 1920s and late 1960s, for example, have tended to produce more "questioned stocks" than periods of less erratic stock price movement. This is not to suggest, however, that all of these companies do not survive.

A good example of this is Ms. Massé's first find. Back in the late sixties, she was papering a wall in her living room with "worthless" stock certificates. One of these belonged to a friend whose uncle had died and left her the stock. Before permitting herself to put glue on the back of the beautifully engraved document, Ms. Massé decided to look up the background of the stock—namely, Bulolo Gold Dredging Ltd. Her investigation showed that this company had been merged into Placer Development Ltd., and the shares were worth $5000.

The sources of investigation into questioned stocks, as well as the results, are similar regardless of the industry. During the middle and late 1800s, as well as the early 1900s, the stock of railroad and mining companies, to name two, was far more abundant in securities market listings than it is today. The stocks of these companies are no more difficult to trace now than the stocks of more recently active industries, such as aerospace and petroleum. It has been Ms. Massé's experience that older issues of securities are at times easier to trace because there are documented records and catalogued information already on file.

What happens, however, if a shareholder inadvertently loses or destroys his or her stock certificate? All is not lost, according to Ms. Massé, because if some proof exists that the person is indeed a legal shareholder in that particular corporation, a claim can be made. In some cases, people have regained their right of ownership to a security even after thirty years. "There is no hard and fast rule. This is what I've learned: it is always worth trying."

TRACER

The expression "wallpaper" has long been used when referring to stock and bond certificates that are considered valueless or worthless. A man living in St. Petersburg, Florida, however, took it literally when he pasted two "worthless" stock certificates on a wall in his home as a constant reminder of his apparent folly.

In came Tracers Company of America, Inc., whose investigation showed that the shares still had value. The surprised homeowner took a saw, cut around the area covered by the certificates, and delivered the entire chunk of wall to be transferred in New York! He received $18,000 for his trouble.

In 1924, Skip Tracers Company was founded for the purpose of tracking down missing persons on behalf of banks, lawyers, and merchants. As its business expanded and its list of clients grew, the company was renamed Tracers Company of America, Inc., in 1948.*

Some twenty-five years ago, corporations began contacting Tracers asking them to perform a very important service. Over the years many companies were merged with or acquired by other companies and thus lost their own

---

* Its address is 509 Madison Avenue, New York, NY 10022.

identity. The surviving firm was faced with the dilemma of having shareholders of the absorbed company who never tendered their old shares for cash or stock in the new company. In addition, some of these people had dividends due to them that had accrued over time and were being held in escrow.

Tracers took on the task, using a unique approach. They would gather the names of people from lists supplied by the client corporation. These names were then grouped according to the location of the person's last known domicile.

Realizing the opportunity to enlist the aid of the public, Tracers contacted local newspapers in the geographical areas of concern and asked them to print the names of the people in question. The newspapers, seeing this to be a local interest story, obliged. Through this effort, many millions of dollars were restored to the rightful owners.

Another facet of the company's growth appeared at about this time, as related by its president, Ed Goldfader. An individual whose name was not listed in the newspaper, but who had a good imagination and a stock certificate considered to be worthless, decided to contact Tracers in the hope that they could help him. They were in fact able to do so, and this added a new dimension to their business. Tracers has been accumulating records on obscure and obsolete companies for years. Their library now contains information on thousands of such companies, and they are very actively engaged in this field, as the following examples illustrate.

THE DOCTOR'S LIBRARY[1]

A physician in Westchester County, New York, came to R. M. Smythe & Company some years ago and asked for a block of worthless securities with which to decorate the walls of his library. Smythe sold him a batch, including stock of a defunct coal company in Pennsylvania, for $40.

About a year later a stranger came to Smythe, asking him if he could locate outstanding shares of the coal company and explaining that oil had been struck on the properties. He was willing to pay heavily for the privilege of canceling the stock bought by the Westchester physician.

The two went to the home of the suburban doctor, and there Smythe stood while the representative of the company thumped a cancellation stamp along the wall of the library and paid $40,000 for the privilege.

THE ENGINEER'S WINDFALL[2]

In the 1950s, a gentleman from Miami, an engineer, had purchased stock in five different uranium mining companies. His belief, like that of many other people, was that uranium was the future of the world.

As his stocks, one by one, disappeared from listing, he felt all was lost. As it turned out, four of them were indeed worthless. One of them, however, Sabre-Pinon Corpora-

---

[1] Anecdote courtesy of R. M. Smythe & Company.
[2] Anecdote courtesy of Micheline Massé.

tion, was merged into United Nuclear, and his shares were worth in excess of $35,000!

THE NUDIST'S CERTIFICATES[3]

A long-time member of a nudist colony discovered that the certificates he owned were valuable. The funds he received were ironically invested in a clothing company.

THE BAKER'S ESTATE

It was over forty years ago that a New York City baker bought approximately $10,000 worth of stock in a utility company. Due to varying economic conditions at that time the utility found the going rough, omitted its dividend, and ceased to be quoted in the financial journals.

When the baker died, he left the certificates as part of his estate to his widow, who assumed them to be worthless. She kept them, however, for sentimental reasons.

The baker's estate, aside from these certificates, was obviously not very substantial, because over the years his widow had to take numerous odd jobs in order to pay her rent and buy food. During this period, and unknown to the widow, the utility merged with another company and once again flourished.

In order to update its records, the utility hired Tracers Company to track down its missing stockholders. The woman was found, informed of the situation, and asked to

---

[3] Anecdote courtesy of Ed Goldfader.

bring her certificates in to the utility for identification and transfer. At first she was skeptical, but *after borrowing carfare*, she appeared at the treasurer's office of the utility and presented her certificates. The stock was worth $66,000.

THE LUCKY SCHOOLTEACHER

Some time ago, a retired schoolteacher wanted to buy shares in a small speculative issue. After considering alternate investment strategies with her broker, she decided to invest part of her assets—a few thousand dollars—by purchasing 1000 shares of the Metals & Controls Company. Subsequently the woman lost track of her investment, because the stock was no longer quoted.

Several years ago, a lawyer advised her to seek the assistance of a professional investigating firm (Tracers), which was able to determine that the stock she held was of a predecessor company to Texas Instruments. On a share-for-share basis, her investment was now worth in excess of a quarter of a million dollars.

THE WOMAN WHO CHANGED HER MIND

One day while going over some old papers, a woman living on social security came across some certificates of stock which she had planned to burn. Fortunately she exercised the privilege of changing her mind, and instead of destroying the certificates she decided to have them investigated.

To her complete joy and surprise, the investigation determined that her stock was worth approximately $7000.

As the story was told, the woman had once also changed her mind about taking an ocean voyage to Europe. The ship she was to sail on was the *Lusitania*!

DIG DEEP

Back in 1860 men were pouring into the newly discovered oil regions of Pennsylvania. Edwin Drake had sunk the first oil well. That magic word "petroleum" was running like a traveling fuse through the land, as that other magic word "gold" did in '49. And over every farm and along every creek in Crawford and Venango Counties the oil hunters swarmed with their little wooden derricks.

Companies were organized by the score, and while the drillers were busy boring for petroleum around Oil City, the nimble-tongued stock salesmen were knocking on doors everywhere, boring for money. Every cornfield, every backyard was snapped up by the promoters, and before the pipe for the well was delivered on the land, the oil shares were on the market.

Some people struck oil and became rich. More struck nothing but gravel and hard luck. One group of promoters took over a remote farm, sold stock certificates in the very neighborhood of Oil City, put down their well, and found their old farm as dry as the desert. They quietly folded their tents, stole away, and forgot all about the beautiful certificates they had issued. The stockholders in Venango County put their stock certificates into old cupboards, wallets, chests, trunks, and china bowls or what-nots. And in the course of time they, too, forgot about them.

The old corporation had been dead for almost sixty

years when one day a gentleman walked into a small, old-fashioned office in the Produce Exchange in New York. He called to see a man who deals in ancient and obsolete securities. (If there is a corporation in its grave anywhere in the world, this man knows it.) His caller was in search of information about the old oil company of 1860 which had died aborning at Oil City. What had become of it? Where were its stockholders? Could they be located? In short, the gentleman, after all these years, wanted to buy the stock.

The dealer in obsolete securities thought he could get the stock. He went to Oil City and in a short time had rounded up and bought every outstanding share in that company—3800 of them. After all those years the holders or their heirs were paid something for their stock, and the security dealer was well paid for his trouble.

What had happened to that stock? Well, in those early days men sent their wells down 20, 30, or 40 feet. Those pioneers were just scraping off the surface oil. Indeed, oil in those days was floating on the waters of the creeks and brooks around Oil City. When the gushers failed to gush after a pipe had been sunk 40 feet, the adventurers concluded there was no oil and ended their adventure. But in these more knowledgeable days of 1929, wells were sent down 1000, 2000 feet, and a group of new prospectors had decided there was oil in that old farm at the deeper levels. They wanted those stock certificates because they wanted to own the corporation which still held title to the farm. When they got it, they put their well down 1400 feet, and up came the rich black flood which the earlier seekers had sought in vain.

The point of the story is clear: Do not assume anything

to be worthless by merely scratching the surface. As with the prospectors who were willing to try alternative methods to capitalize on a venture considered valueless, the narrative suggests that fortunes have been discovered by those who *dig deep*.

CHAPTER THREE

THE
INVESTIGATION: I

The vast majority of companies, both large and small, do not disappear without a trace. Somewhere records are kept, and by following the steps set forth in Chapters 3 and 4, which constitute the "meat" of this book, results should be obtained. There will not be a pot of gold waiting at the end of the rainbow in all cases, unfortunately; but if the status of questioned stocks can finally be determined one way or the other, the search will have accomplished its objective.

RECOMMENDED PROCEDURE

In any investigative procedure a logical and orderly approach is necessary, and Figure 3-1 illustrates a typical course of action. Following this outline, we first "identify the problem"—i.e., a questioned stock. The next step is to gather as much information as possible.

STARTING POINT: THE CERTIFICATE ITSELF

The primary source of most of the information that you will need to begin your investigation will be the face of your stock certificate (see Figure 3-2 for a sample). This certificate is either in your possession or held by your broker. If it is held by your broker, it is most likely to be in "street name," that is, it is carried in the name of the brokerage firm or in the name of the prior owner, but in either case held strictly for your account. In this case, have your broker send the certificate to you as soon as possible. On the face of your certificate you will find the following items that are essential to your investigation:

1. FULL LEGAL NAME AND EXACT SPELLING OF THE CORPORATION

The name is established at the time of incorporation by the filling of the company's charter. This will become very important, especially in the investigation of smaller or older companies, since many of them will have very similar names.

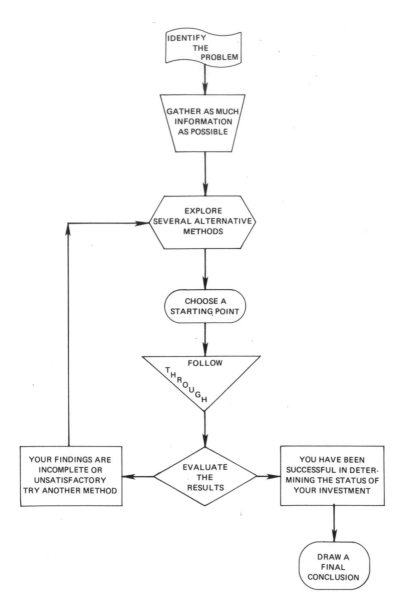

Figure 3-1   Sequence of steps for an investigation.

Figure 3-2 A typical stock certificate.

2. STATE AND DATE OF INCORPORATION

Since thousands of corporations have been formed over the years, it is common to find more than one company with the same name; however, they are usually incorporated in different states at different times. Based upon this fact, the state and date of incorporation become vital to your search. This information, along with the corporate name, comprises the corporate seal.

3. IDENTIFYING NUMBER OF THE STOCK CERTIFICATE

This number is used by the company for issuing, transferring, record-keeping, and cross-referencing purposes. To the holder of the certificate, this number can be of significance for additional identification purposes.

4. NUMBER OF SHARES OWNED

This will appear on your stock certificate both in numerals and in written words, just as with a check. Newer certificates use a perforation system in addition to words and numbers.

5. NAME OF LEGAL OWNER

The stock will probably be registered in the name of the purchaser. In the event you received the stock in street name, as mentioned earlier, the stock may be registered in your broker's name or in the name of the previous owner. In this case, the stock will be stamped transferable to you as the owner. The back of the stock certificate is used for this purpose. In the case of inherited securities, either ownership has been transferred to the present owner's name, or proof of ownership is available via probate. As a point of information, the stockholder whose name appears on the face of the stock certificate is known as the *stockholder of record* on the books of the issuing corporation. This may or may not be the beneficial owner of the shares (as in the case of street name stock), that is, the owner who actually receives the benefits of stock ownership, such as dividends, capital appreciation, and voting rights, to name a few.

6. DATE OF ISSUE

This represents the date that the stock was last transferred on the books and records of the corporation into the name of the owner of record, which appears on the face of the certificate. This date does not always denote the time of the purchase, since a stock acquired many years ago could have been held in street name and transferred some time later. In any event, this date will be very helpful in your search because it will indicate that at that time the stock of the corporation was being transferred. Companies do not have to be actively engaged in their particular operation in order for their stock to be bought or sold. The date of issue, however, is an important reference point in your investigation and will be further explained in a later procedure.

7. NAMES OF OFFICERS AND THEIR TITLES

Each stock certificate must be signed by at least two duly authorized officers of the corporation. The corporate charter designates which officers have this power, as well as their titles. In most cases, it will be the president and the secretary of the corporation.

Depending upon the age of the certificates, the size of the corporation, and the volume of trading, these signatures can be either individually signed or preprinted.

8. TRANSFER AGENT

The transfer agent's function is a very important one. The responsibilities include transferring stock that has been bought or sold, keeping track of the names and addresses of current stockholders, and issuing proxy notices.

This service is usually handled by a commercial bank or trust company, but it can be done by an independent transfer agency or by the company itself. The name and location of the transfer agent can be found on the face of the stock certificate.

9. REGISTRAR

The function of the registrar is to see to it that all stock issued is valid and in compliance with the corporate charter as sanctioned by the company's particular state of incorporation. It is the registrar's responsibility, for example, to prevent the issuance of more stock than has been authorized. This task is usually administered by a commercial bank or trust company, whose name and location can be found on the certificate.

10. PAR VALUE

This figure represents the dollar amount assigned to each share of stock (both common and preferred) in accordance with the charter of the corporation.

For bookkeeping and transfer tax purposes, a corporation may issue stock with no par value assigned to it and instead assign a *stated value*. In either case, it will be so stated on the face of the stock certificate.

The information gathered from the certificate is all that you need to begin your investigation.

SOURCES OF FURTHER INFORMATION

The next step is to explore several alternative methods. Ten sources, most of which independently may determine the status of your investment, are listed here. The first four can be used without gathering any additional information.

1. The Secretary of State

2. The Securities and Exchange Commission

3. The Transfer Agent and Registrar

4. The National Association of Securities Dealers

The fifth method may require you to compile some additional information, and the method of doing so will be fully outlined later in the text.

5. The Company and/or Officers directly

Sources 6 through 10 require a visit to the business book section of the public library.

6. R. M. Smythe & Co., Inc.

7. Financial Information, Inc.—*Directory of Obsolete Securities*

8. *The National Stock Summary*

9. News media

10. Other sources of information

After a review of these methods the investigator should now choose a starting point, follow through, and evaluate the results.

THE SECRETARY OF STATE

The branch of state government empowered to create corporations is the Office of the Secretary of State. Any person or group wishing to conduct business as a corporation must file a certificate of incorporation with this office. Upon acceptance and approval by the Office of the Secretary of State, the certificate of incorporation becomes the *corporate charter*, or *articles of incorporation*.

The corporate charter usually includes the official name of the corporation, the names of the officers and directors, the company's line of business, capitalization, corporate headquarters, and other such pertinent information. At this point, a corporation is recognized as a legal entity under the laws governing that particular charter, is recognized as engaging in an appropriate business venture, and, for all practical purposes, is recognized as a person. It can enter into contractual agreements, it can sue or be sued, it can live or die.

If the company is still in existence on the books and records of the Office of the Secretary of State of the state of incorporation that appears on the corporate seal found on your stock certificate, any of the above information that is on file with this office is available to the general public upon request.

Cancellation of a corporate charter is effected by either (1) revocation by the state or (2) voluntary forfeiture by the company.

Nonpayment of taxes, proven fraud, and an adjudicated bankruptcy are some examples of why the state would revoke a charter. Revocation of a corporate charter by the Office of the Secretary of State is public information, and the exact reason and date of occurrence can be made available to you.

Voluntary liquidation, that is, a corporate decision to dissolve a business venture by liquidating the assets, paying off the liabilities, and distributing the remainder (if any) to the shareholders, is an example of forfeiture. Refiling of a company's corporate charter in another location for tax purposes or reasons of proximity is another.

Some states do not require a reason as to why a corporation forfeits its charter; however, in all states the date of this occurrence is available.

Listed alphabetically according to state on the following pages are the offices of the secretaries of state with their mailing addresses and phone numbers. Some states require a fee, and the amount will be listed. In order to expedite matters when contacting the Office of the Secretary of State by mail (see Figure 3-3, which may also serve as a guide for a telephone inquiry), you should include a self-

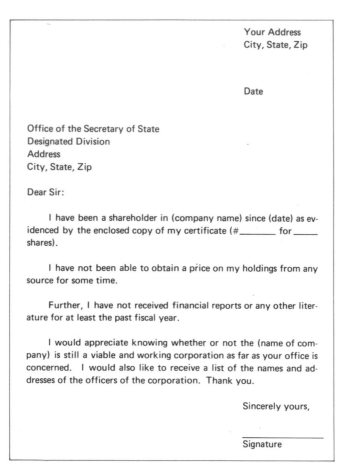

Figure 3-3   Sample letter to the Secretary of State.

addressed, stamped envelope, your check made payable to the Office of the Secretary of State or as otherwise noted on the list, and a photocopy of the face of your stock certificate. *Do not send cash; do not send the original certificate.*

ALABAMA
State Department of
Revenue,
Franchise Tax Division
Montgomery, AL 36100
(205) 832-6855

ALASKA
Department of
Commerce
Office of the
Commissioner
Juneau, AK 99801
(907) 465-3520

ARIZONA
Arizona Corporation
Commission
Incorporating Division
Capitol Annex
1688 West Adams Street
Phoenix, AZ 85000
Fee: $1; check to order of
Arizona Corporation
Commission
(602) 271-4286

ARKANSAS
Office of the Secretary of
State
Corporation Department
Little Rock, AR 72201
(501) 374-1628

CALIFORNIA
Office of the Secretary
of State

Corporation Department
Sacramento, CA 95814
(916) 445-6371

COLORADO
Office of the Secretary
of State
127 Capitol Building
Denver, CO 80200
(303) 892-3301

CONNECTICUT
Office of the Secretary
of State
Corporation Division
Hartford, CT 06100
(203) 566-4346

DELAWARE
Office of the Secretary
of State
Corporation Department
Dover, DE 19901
Fee: $5
(302) 678-4111

DISTRICT OF COLUMBIA
Office of the Recorder
of Deeds
Corporation Division
6th & D Streets, N.W.
Washington, DC 20001
(202) 347-0671

FLORIDA
Office of the Secretary
The Capitol

Tallahassee, FL 32304
Attn: Corporations
  Division
Up to 3 requests, no
  charge
(904) 488-3140

GEORGIA
  Office of the Secretary
    of State
  Atlanta, GA 30334
  (404) 656-2881

HAWAII
  State of Hawaii
  Business Registration
    Division
  Department of
    Regulatory Agencies
  Post Office Box 40
  Honolulu, HI 96800
  (808) 548-2544

IDAHO
  Office of the Secretary
    of State
  Boise, ID 83700
  (208) 384-2300

ILLINOIS
  Office of the Secretary
    of State
  Corporation Division
  Springfield, IL 62706
  Fee: $2
  (217) 782-7880

INDIANA
  Office of the Secretary
    of State
  Corporation Records
    Department
  Indianapolis, IN 46200
  (317) 733-6531

IOWA
  Office of the Secretary
    of State
  Corporation Records
    Department
  Des Moines, IA 50300
  (515) 281-5864

KANSAS
  Office of the Secretary
    of State
  Second Floor
  State Capitol Building
  Topeka, KS 66603
  (913) 296-2236

KENTUCKY
  Office of the Secretary
    of State
  Frankfort, KY 40601
  (502) 564-3490

LOUISIANA
  Office of the Secretary
    of State
  Post Office Box 4125
  Baton Rouge, LA 70804
  (504) 389-6181

MAINE
Office of the Secretary
of State
Corporation Division
Augusta, ME 04330
(207) 289-3676

MARYLAND
State Department of
Assessments and
Taxation
301 West Preston Street
Baltimore, MD 21201
(301) 267-5424

MASSACHUSETTS
Office of the Secretary,
Commonwealth of
Massachusetts
Corporations Division
State House
Boston, MA 02133
Fee: $1
(617) 727-2850

MICHIGAN
Office of the Secretary
of State
Corporation and
Securities Commission
300 East Michigan
Avenue
Lansing, MI 48900
(517) 373-6610

MINNESOTA
Office of the Secretary
of State

Corporations Division
State Capitol Building
St. Paul, MN 55101
(612) 296-3266

MISSISSIPPI
Office of the Secretary
of State
Securities Division
Post Office Box 136
Jackson, MS 39200
(601) 354-6541

MISSOURI
Office of the Secretary
of State
Correspondence
Supervisor
Corporation Department
Jefferson City, MO 65101
Fee: $1
(314) 751-2331

MONTANA
Office of the Secretary
of State
Capitol
Helena, MT 59601
Fee: $2
(406) 449-2034

NEBRASKA
Office of the Secretary
of State
Corporation Division
State Capitol Building
Lincoln, NE 68509
(402) 471-2556

NEVADA
Deputy Secretary of State
Carson City, NV 89701
(702) 885-5203

NEW HAMPSHIRE
Office of the Secretary
of State
Room 204
State House
Concord, NH 03301
(603) 271-1110

NEW JERSEY
Office of the Secretary
of State
State House,
Trenton, NJ 08625
Fee: $5
(609) 292-2121

NEW MEXICO
State Corporation
Commission
Corporation Department
Post Office Drawer 1269
Santa Fe, NM 87501
(505) 827-2717

NEW YORK
Division of Corporations
and State Records
162 Washington Avenue
Albany, NY 12224
(518) 474-2121

NORTH CAROLINA
Office of the Secretary
of State
Raleigh, NC 27602
(919) 829-3433

NORTH DAKOTA
Office of the Secretary
of State
Capitol Building
Bismark, ND 58501
Fee: $2
(701) 224-2900

OHIO
Office of the Secretary
of State
Corporation Department
State Capitol Building
Columbus, OH 43200
(614) 466-4980

OKLAHOMA
Office of the Secretary
of State
Corporation Records
Department
Oklahoma City, OK 73109
(405) 521-3911

OREGON
Corporation Division
Department of
Commerce
301 Labor and Industries
Building
Salem, OR 97301
(503) 378-4139

PENNSYLVANIA
Office of the Secretary
Commonwealth of
Pennsylvania
Corporation Bureau
Post Office Box 551
Harrisburg, PA 17100
Fee: $0.50
(717) 787-7630

PUERTO RICO
Office of the Secretary
of State
Department of State
Commonwealth of
Puerto Rico
San Juan, PR 00900

RHODE ISLAND
Office of the Secretary
of State
Corporation Division
Room 219
State Office Building
Providence, RI 02900
(401) 277-3040

SOUTH CAROLINA
Office of the Secretary
of State
Department of State
Columbia, SC 29211
(803) 758-2744

SOUTH DAKOTA
Office of the Secretary
of State

Department of State
Pierre, SD 57501
(605) 224-3537

TENNESSEE
Office of the Secretary
of State
Nashville, TN 37200
(615) 741-2816

TEXAS
Office of the Secretary
of State
Corporation Division
Austin, TX 78711
Fee: $1
(512) 475-2015

UTAH
Office of the Secretary
of State
Corporation Clerk
Room 203
State Capitol Building
Salt Lake City, UT 84100
(801) 533-5151

VERMONT
Office of the Secretary
of State
c/o Corporation Clerk
Montpelier, VT 05602
(802) 828-2363

VIRGINIA
Clerk of the State Cor-
poration Commission

Commonwealth of
Virginia
Box 1197
Richmond, VA 23209
(804) 770-2441

WASHINGTON
Office of the Secretary
of State
Supervisor of
Corporations
Olympia, WA 98501
(206) 753-3550

WEST VIRGINIA
Office of the Secretary
of State

Department of State
Charleston, WV 25311
(304) 348-2112

WISCONSIN
Office of the Secretary
of State
Corporation Division
Madison, WI 53700
Fee: $2
(608) 266-3590

WYOMING
Office of the Secretary
of State
Cheyenne, WY 82001
(307) 777-7378

CANADIAN PROVINCES

ALBERTA
Department of the
Provincial Secretary
Registrar of Companies
Room 205
Legislative Building
Edmonton, Alta.,
Canada
Fee: $1

BRITISH COLUMBIA
Registrar of Companies
Law Courts
850 Burdett Avenue
Victoria, B.C., Canada
Fee: $0.50

MANITOBA
Companies Branch
Department of the
Provincial Secretary
Legislative Building
Winnipeg 1, Man.,
Canada
Fee: $1

NEW BRUNSWICK
Deputy Provincial
Secretary
Fredericton, N.B.
Canada
Fee: $1

NEWFOUNDLAND
Registry of Companies
Office
Confederation Building
St. John's, Nfld., Canada
Fee: $1

NOVA SCOTIA
Registrar of Joint Stock
Companies
Province House
Post Office Box 1529
Halifax, N.S., Canada
Fee: $0.50

ONTARIO
Department of the
Provincial Secretary
and Citizenship
Supervisor of Records
Companies Branch
Parliament Buildings
Toronto, Ont., Canada
Fee: $2

PRINCE EDWARD ISLAND
Prince Edward Island

Provincial Secretary
Administrative Assistant
Charlottetown, P.E.I.,
Canada

QUEBEC
Director of Companies
Branch
Provincial Secretary's
Department
Parliament Building
Quebec 1, Que., Canada

SASKATCHEWAN
Registrar of Joint Stock
Companies
Legislative Building
Sask., Canada
Fee: $0.50

YUKON TERRITORY
Registrar of Joint Stock
Companies
Government of Yukon
Territory
Whitehorse, Yukon,
Canada

CARIBBEAN AND CENTRAL AMERICA

BAHAMAS
Registrar General's
Office
Nassau, Bahamas, B.W.I.
Fee: $0.75 (U.S.)

PANAMA
Direccion Registro
Publico
Ministerio de Justicia
Apartado 3452
Panama City, Panama

with the commission are available for inspection in the Public Reference Room of the commission's headquarters office in Washington, DC. Copies of portions or all of any such public document may be obtained. Estimates as to the cost of copies of specific reports or other information may be obtained on request to the Section of Public Reference, Office of Records and Service, Securities and Exchange Commission, Washington, DC 20549.

Current annual and other periodic reports (including financial statements) filed by companies whose securities are listed on exchanges are also available for inspection in the commission's New York, Chicago, and San Francisco regional offices, as are the registration statements (and subsequent reports) filed by those companies whose securities are traded over the counter which register under the 1964 Amendments to the Exchange Act. Moreover, if the issuer's principal office is located in the area served by the Atlanta, Boston, Denver, Fort Worth, or Seattle regional office, its filings also may be examined at the particular regional office in question. In addition, prospectuses covering recent public offerings of securities registered under the Securities Act may be examined by contacting regional offices; and copies of broker-dealer and investment adviser registrations, as well as Regulation A notifications and offering circulars, may be examined in the particular regional office in which they were filed.

In order to help you expedite your inquiry to the SEC, the following information is included:

1.   A listing of the regional and branch offices of the

commission, including their addresses, and the names of the regional administrators in charge.

2. A map (Figure 3-4) showing the headquarters, regional offices, and branch offices of the SEC, along with the registered and exempt exchanges.

3. A sample letter (Figure 3-5) to serve as an outline when contacting the SEC by mail; it can also be helpful as a guide for a phone inquiry.

REGIONAL OFFICES AND REGIONAL ADMINISTRATORS IN CHARGE

ATLANTA
Jule B. Greene
Suite 138
1375 Peachtree Street, N.E.
Atlanta, GA 30309

BOSTON
Floyd H. Gilbert
150 Causeway Street
Boston, MA 02114

CHICAGO
William D. Goldsberry
Room 1708
Everett McKinley
   Dirksen Building
219 South Dearborn
   Street
Chicago, IL 60604

DENVER
Robert H. Davenport
Two Park Central
1515 Arapahoe Street
Denver, CO 80202

FORT WORTH
Richard M. Hewitt
503, U.S. Courthouse
10th & Lamar Streets
Fort Worth, TX 76102

LOS ANGELES
Gerald E. Boltz
10960 Wilshire Blvd.
U.S. Courthouse
312 North Spring Street
Los Angeles, CA 90024

NEW YORK
William D. Moran

26 Federal Plaza
New York, NY 10007

SAN FRANCISCO
Leonard H. Rossen
450 Golden Gate Avenue
Box 36042
San Francisco, CA 94102

SEATTLE
Jack H. Bookey

Room 810
915 2nd Avenue
Seattle, WA 98174

WASHINGTON, DC
Paul F. Leonard
Room 306
Ballston Center Tower
No. 3
4015 Wilson Boulevard
Arlington, VA 22203

BRANCH OFFICES

CLEVELAND
Room 899
Federal Office Building
1240 East 9th at Lakeside
Cleveland, OH 44199

DETROIT
1044 Federal Building
Detroit, MI 48226

HOUSTON
7615 Federal Office &
Courts Building
515 Rusk Avenue
Houston, TX 77002

MIAMI
Suite 701
Dupont Plaza Center

300 Biscayne Boulevard
Way
Miami, FL 33131

PHILADELPHIA
600 Arch Street
Room 2204
Federal Building
Philadelphia, PA 19106

SALT LAKE CITY
Federal Reserve Bank
Building
Room 6004
120 South State Street
Salt Lake City, UT 84111

ST. LOUIS
Room 1452
210 North Twelfth Street
St. Louis, MO 63101

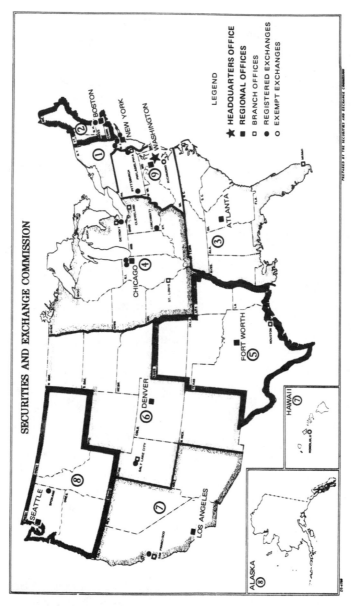

Figure 3-4   Headquarters, regional offices, and branch offices of the SEC.

Your Address
City, State, Zip
Date

Securities & Exchange Commission
Proper Regional or Branch Office
Address
City, State, Zip

Attention: Administrator in Charge

Dear Sirs:

    I have been a shareholder in (company name) since (date) as evidenced by the enclosed copy of my certificate (# _____) for (_____) shares.

    I have not been able to obtain a price on my holdings from any source for some time.

    Further, I have not received financial reports or any other literature for at least the past fiscal year.

    I would appreciate knowing whether or not the corporation has been suspended in trading by your office, and if so, the reason why. Thank you.

Sincerely yours,

_____
Signature

encl.

Figure 3-5 Sample letter to the SEC.

THE TRANSFER AGENT AND REGISTRAR

The companies providing these services are probably the last to have processed the stock certificate that is in question. Having obtained the name and location of the transfer agent and registrar from the face of your stock certificate, you can contact them by mail or phone, directing your inquiry to the attention of the Stock Transfer Department. These agencies may be able to provide for you the last date that shares of your particular company were transferred and verified on the books and records of the corporation.

In some instances, the transfer agent is also the trustee; that is, a fiduciary relationship exists whereby one party holds something of value for the benefit of another—in this case, funds from a liquidated corporation for distribution to its shareholders.

Occasionally, the services of the transfer agent and registrar will be performed by the same commercial bank, trust company, or independent agent, or by the corporation itself.

THE NATIONAL ASSOCIATION OF SECURITIES DEALERS

The National Association of Securities Dealers, commonly known as the NASD, is a voluntary association of broker/dealers organized in 1939 under authority granted by the Maloney Act, an amendment to the Securities Exchange Act of 1934. The stated objectives of the NASD, as they apply to broker/dealers, are to:

1. Promote standardization of principles and practices.

2. Promote high standards of commercial honor.

3.   Provide liaison with governmental agencies.

4.   Adopt, administer, and enforce rules of fair practice.

5.   Promote self-discipline among members.

This organization oversees the vast over-the-counter securities market and in doing so, among its other very important functions, keeps huge amounts of records and information regarding the companies under its jurisdiction.

Research activities are exhaustively and completely conducted, and they cover such valuable information as:

1.   Financial statements

2.   Past and current status of securities (mergers, acquisitions, changes in management, etc.)

3.   Trading activity

Inquiries regarding securities traded in the over-the-counter market should be directed to:

Customer Inquiries
National Association of Securities Dealers
77 Water Street
New York, NY 10005
(212) 344-7690

A letter such as the one suggested to contact the Securities and Exchange Commission (Figure 3-5) can be used.

CONTACTING THE COMPANY AND ITS OFFICERS DIRECTLY

Using the corporate address found in the *National Stock Summary* or obtained through the Office of the Secretary of State, you may direct inquiries to your company's Stockholder Relations Department or to the Secretary of the Corporation. (Figure 3-6 gives a general-purpose guide.) Provide the company with as much information and proof of ownership as possible. This can be easily accomplished by including with your letter a photocopy of the face of your stock certificate. In the case of "street name" or inherited stocks, include copies of both sides of the certificate.

In your letter you should inform the company of the fact that you have not been able to obtain any recent price quotes or financial information. Also state that you expect to receive from them complete details on the status of your investment.

This method should also be used when contacting an officer or director of the corporation, whose names and resident addresses can be obtained from the Office of the Secretary of State if this information is available.

Different states have different rules regarding incorporation. Some states do not require that a corporation file the names and resident addresses of its officers and/or directors and, therefore, cannot give you that particular information.

However, there are other sources which can be explored. Some of the major investment advisory publications, which can be found in the library, banks, and brokerage firms, report the names of corporate officers and/or

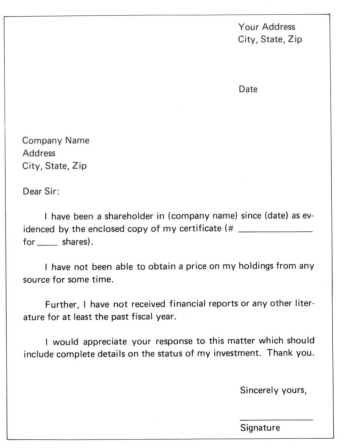

Your Address
City, State, Zip

Date

Company Name
Address
City, State, Zip

Dear Sir:

I have been a shareholder in (company name) since (date) as evidenced by the enclosed copy of my certificate (# _____ for ____ shares).

I have not been able to obtain a price on my holdings from any source for some time.

Further, I have not received financial reports or any other literature for at least the past fiscal year.

I would appreciate your response to this matter which should include complete details on the status of my investment. Thank you.

Sincerely yours,

_____
Signature

Figure 3-6 Sample letter contacting the company directly.

directors. The Standard & Poor Corporation, for example, lists these names in its *Corporation Register* and *Stock Reports*, which are commonly referred to as "tear sheets."

Another method of obtaining this information is to find past issues of your company's Annual Report, 10-K Statement, prospectus, news releases, and other corporate literature which may still be on file or microfilm in libraries, brokerage firms, the stock exchanges, or the Securities and Exchange Commission.

The names obtained through any of the above means, as well as from the face of the stock certificate, will need addresses and/or telephone numbers to be of significant value. More often than not, a corporate official will reside fairly close to corporate headquarters. It may be worth while to check with telephone directory assistance or the post offices in the area surrounding the company's corporate headquarters.

CHAPTER FOUR

THE INVESTIGATION: II

The previous chapter discussed the major sources that one should contact when trying to determine the status of questioned stocks. We now describe several other important sources of information concerning securities. In most cases the methods outlined here will require a visit to the business book section of your local public library.

R. M. SMYTHE & COMPANY, INC.

This company* has been in the business of identifying obsolete securities for nearly a century. In 1904, the firm published *Obsolete American Securities and Corporations*, which was the first book in this field.

Today, aside from being involved in many other security-oriented activities, this prestigious firm publishes the *Robert D. Fisher Manual of Valuable and Worthless Securities*, which contains a list of valuable, extinct, or obsolete securities. The forerunner of this publication is the *Marvyn Scudder Manual of Extinct or Obsolete Companies*, which covers the first four volumes in the series (up to 1934). These reference manuals are available in the business book section of major libraries.

The following selections taken from the *Robert D. Fisher Manual of Valuable and Worthless Securities* have been selected to emphasize the reporting techniques of this service:

MARCONI WIRELESS TELEGRAPH COMPANY OF AMERICA (N.J.)
Common stock. Acquired by R.C.A. in 1919. Unstamped stock is entitled to shares of Radio Corporation of America, 30 Rockefeller Plaza, New York. Each share is exchangeable for 1 share R.C.A. common stock and $5.50 in cash. Stamped stock became worthless in 1943.

IRVAN FERROMAGNETICS CORP. (CALIF.)
All equipment was repossessed under chattel mortgage.

---

* R. M. Smythe & Co., Inc., 170 Broadway, New York, NY 10038.

Little or no assets remained, and no petition of bankruptcy was filed. The case was closed on August 9, 1963 by a representative for the company's creditors.

COMO MINES COMPANY (NEV. 1929)
Adjudicated bankrupt on August 5, 1936 by Federal District Court, Reno, Nevada. In 1938 the company reorganized, and "old" stock called in for "new" stock on the basis of 5 old for 1 new. Thought for years to be worthless, this stock is good and can be transferred. The address of [transfer agent] is Nevada Agency & Trust Co., Reno, Nevada. The company owns a number of patented and unpatented mining claims in the Como Mining District near Virginia City, Nevada.

CONNECTICUT GAS & COKE SECURITIES CO. (CONN.)
Each share of Preferred received 1⅗ shares of New Haven Gas Light Company and 4/25 shares of Hartford Gas Company at the Union & New Haven Trust Co. in New Haven. Shares not exchanged before 2/15/53 became null and void. There was no provision made for holders of Common stock.

FLEETWOOD AIRFLOW, INC. (PA. 1942)
The company was incorporated in 1942 as Laux Manufacturing Company. In October 1945 the name was changed to Fleetwood Industries, Inc. In January 1946 the name of the company was changed again to Fleetwood Airflow Inc., location Wilkes-Barre, Pa. On September 1, 1951 we were advised by a source that the company was bankrupt. No $ value found for the Capital stock, 50¢ par.

FLORIDA DOWNS, INC. (FLA. 1946)
The former name was Sunshine Park Racing Association

Inc., which changed its name to the above on 12/28/65. Florida Downs, Inc. was dissolved in November 1967. A liquidating dividend of $2.033 per share Common stock can be obtained by forwarding the shares to the Marine Bank & Trust Co., 315 Madison Ave., Tampa, Fla.

These volumes contain many thousands of examples of questioned stocks.

THE DIRECTORY OF OBSOLETE SECURITIES

One of the most useful tools that can be employed in the investigation of a questioned stock is a very highly developed manual entitled *The Directory of Obsolete Securities*.[1]

This publication lists many thousands of questioned stocks along with a comment on the current status of each, as well as the state of incorporation, classes of securities, and important dates.

Financial Information, Inc., a prominent firm with over fifty years of research and investigative experience, publishes *The Directory of Obsolete Securities* annually. This yearly update is designed to provide current, accurate, and reliable information.

Although this firm deals exclusively with institutions (banks, brokerage houses, trust companies, etc.) and does not solicit from or sell its services to the general public, copies of its publication can be found in the business book section of public libraries.

---

[1] Published by Financial Information, Inc., 170 Varick Street, New York, NY 10013 (Stephen J. Kappel, Publisher).

From *The Directory of Obsolete Securities* some selected examples have been chosen to depict the exhaustive efforts that each year go into its publication:[2]

ACF-WRIGLEY STORES, INC. (DEL.)
Name changed to Allied Supermarkets, Inc. 11/10/61.

A M I, INC. (MICH.)
Recapitalized under the laws of Delaware 1/2/52.
Each share 6% Preferred $20 par exchanged for (4) shares Common no par.
Each share Common $5 par exchanged for (1) share Common no par.
A M I, Inc. (Del.) merged into Automatic Canteen Co. of America 3/27/59.
Automatic Canteen Co. of America name changed to Canteen Corp. 2/16/66, which merged into International Telephone & Telegraph Corp. (Del.) 4/25/69.

ABACUS FUND (MASS.)
Reincorporated under the laws of Delaware as Abacus Fund, Inc. 3/31/64.
Abacus Fund, Inc. merged into Paine, Webber, Jackson & Curtis Inc. 4/3/72, which reorganized as Paine Webber Inc. 2/1/74.

ABRAHAM & STRAUS, INC.
Acquired by Federated Department Stores, Inc. in 1949.
Each share Common no par exchanged for (3.25) shares Common $5 par.

---

[2] © 1978, Financial Information, Inc.

ALMADEN VINEYARDS, INC. (DEL.)
(Common 10¢)
Merged into National Distillers & Chemical Corp. 6/30/77.
Each share Common 10¢ par exchanged for $12.25 cash.

ALPHA BETA FOOD MARKETS, INC. (CALIF.)
Each share Common $10 par exchanged for (2.5) shares
Common $1 par in 1956.
Under plan of merger each share 5% Preferred A $10 par
exchanged for (2.5) shares 6% Preferred $25 par 5/27/59,
which was subsequently called for redemption 11/25/60.
Merger into American Stores Co. 1/16/61.
Each share Common $1 par exchanged for (0.277778) share
Common $1 par.
American Stores Co. name changed to Acme Markets, Inc.
6/28/62, which name changed back to American Stores Co.
12/29/73.

AMERADA CORP. (DEL.)
Name changed to Amerada Petroleum Corp. 12/24/41.
Amerada Petroleum Corp. merged into Amerada Hess Corp.
6/20/69.

AMECHE-GINO FOODS, INC. (MD.)
Name changed to A-G Foods, Inc. 5/3/62.
A-G Foods, Inc. name changed to Gino's Inc. 4/3/69.

AMERICAN BANTAM CAR CO. (PA.)
Common no par changed to $1 par 6/24/45.
Common $1 par reclassified as Class A $1 par 7/6/48.
Reorganized 1/17/55.
Each share Class A $1 par exchanged for (1) share Common
$1 par.
Class B no par had no equity.
Under plan of merger name changed to Pressed Metals of

America, Inc. (Pa.) and Common $1 par changed to 10¢ par 5/15/56.

Pressed Metals of America, Inc. (Pa.) recapitalized as Klion (H.L.) Inc. (Pa.) 10/17/60, which reincorporated under the laws of New York 10/31/63.

Klion (H.L.) Inc. (N.Y.) acquired by Korvette (E.J.), Inc. 8/23/65, which merged into Spartans Industries, Inc. (N.Y.) 9/25/66, which merged into Arlen Realty & Development Corp. 2/26/71.

THE NATIONAL MONTHLY STOCK SUMMARY

The National Monthly Stock Summary is a very useful and informative reference book published by The National Quotation Bureau Incorporated.[3] Its contents include a summarization of stock market quotations which have appeared in the *National Daily Services* or have been supplied by dealers on special lists. This daily service is commonly known as the "Pink Sheets," so called because it is printed on pink paper and contains a listing of the bid and asked prices of over-the-counter securities as submitted by broker/dealers.

As a point of information, the "Yellow Sheets," published by the same organization, provides the same daily service for bonds and debentures.

On the following pages, The National Quotation Bureau Incorporated has allowed us to reprint from their publication, *The National Monthly Stock Summary*, an example (Figure 4-1).

---

[3] The National Quotation Bureau Incorporated, 116 Nassau Street, New York, NY 10038.

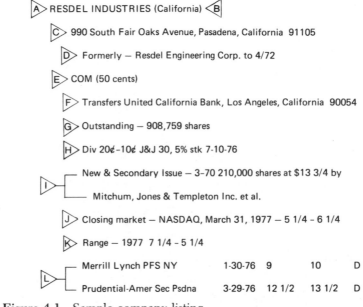

Figure 4-1 Sample company listing.

This reference book, which has been published since 1913, can be found in brokerage houses, commercial banks, trust companies, and the business book section of any public library. It is published semiannually each April and October.

The National Bond Summary, also published semiannually by the National Quotation Bureau Incorporated, is available every January and July. This reference book is similar in scope to *The National Stock Summary*.

AN EXAMPLE: RESDEL INDUSTRIES

This example, taken from page 1178 of the April 1, 1977, issue of *The National Stock Summary*, was carefully chosen to show the information found in this publication which may be used to increase the scope of your investigation.

A. RESDEL INDUSTRIES

Official corporate name as designated by the company's corporate charter.

B. CALIFORNIA

State of incorporation—this designates that the company was incorporated under the laws of the state of California. This does not mean, however, that the company must have its principal place of business in that state or that it must, in fact, conduct any business at all there.

C. 990 SOUTH FAIR OAKS AVENUE, PASADENA, CALIFORNIA 91105

The corporate mailing address, which is usually the company's corporate headquarters. You will note that in this particular example the company maintains its principal place of business in the state of its incorporation. This address can be used to contact the company directly.

D. FORMERLY—RESDEL ENGINEERING CORP. TO 4/72

For a variety of reasons companies may from time to time modify or change completely their official corporate name. In this example we can hypothesize that Resdel had diversified and decided to express these new interests to the public by modifying their corporate name. The actual mechanics of a name change may differ from company to company but usually involve a majority vote of the stockholders and an amendment to the corporate charter. In this case, the official name of the corporation was changed some time in April of 1972.

E.   COM *(50 cents)*

Represents that the company's common stock carries a par value of 50 cents per share. Par value may or may not be assigned to the stock of a corporation (common and/or preferred) under the terms and conditions of the company's corporate charter. In the event that a company does not choose to assign its stock a par value, the representation will appear thus: COM (NO PAR).

F.   TRANSFERS UNITED CALIFORNIA BANK, LOS ANGELES, CALIF. 90054

Discloses the name and principal location of the company's primary transfer agent. Large national corporations whose stock is actively traded can have more than one transfer agent, usually strategically located in different parts of the country.

G.   OUTSTANDING—908,759 SHARES

This figure indicates the number of shares of common stock which the company has outstanding, which is commonly referred to as the *float*. This is not to be confused with the number of common shares that the company is "authorized" to issue under the terms of its corporate charter, which is usually a greater amount. Authorized but as yet unissued stock can be called up for such purposes as secondary offerings (public or private) in order to raise additional capital; acquisitions, whereby the company will acquire the common stock of another company in exchange for new shares of its own common stock; and stock dividends to its present shareholders. Keep in mind that whenever a company issues additional shares of stock, keeping its equity base the same, the result is known as *dilution*. The company's assets, equity, earnings, book value, etc., when stated on a per share basis, decrease. As with the corporate name and par value, a company may increase or decrease its authorized stock by a majority vote of the stockholders and amendment to the corporate charter.

H.   DIV 20¢–10¢ J&J 30, 5% STOCK 7/10/76

A dividend is most commonly a cash distribution to shareholders of a part of the profits earned by the company. Dividends are declared by the Board of Directors and once initiated can be increased, decreased, or totally eliminated, depending upon the fortunes of the company. A corporation can also pay a one-time special cash dividend out of windfall profits. It should be noted that cash dividends can decrease the equity base of the company; as profits are earned they are booked into retained earnings, from which cash dividends are paid.

Companies have the option to issue stock dividends, which are always represented as a percentage. A two-for-one stock split, for example, is in essence a 100% stock dividend. As mentioned earlier, these stock dividends are "paid" from stock that has been authorized by the company's corporate charter but not yet issued and outstanding.

DIV 20-10¢ J&J 30: This statement indicates that the company's current dividend policy is to pay an annual cash dividend to its stockholders of 20 cents per share of common stock. It is payable 10 cents per share on January 30th and 10 cents per share on July 30th of the current fiscal year.

5% STK 7-10-76: This statement indicates that on July 10, 1976, the company paid a 5 percent stock dividend to its shareholders. This transaction increased the total amount of issued and outstanding common stock by 5 percent. Keep in mind that a stock dividend or a stock split does not affect the stockholder's percentage of ownership in the corporation.

In order for a stockholder to be eligible to receive dividends in any form, the company establishes a date known as the *record date*, which is usually before the company announces it has declared a dividend, on which date the stockholder must have been a registered owner.

I.   NEW & SECONDARY ISSUE—3-70 210,000 SHARES AT $13 3/4 BY MITCHUM, JONES & TEMPLETON INC. ET AL.

The initial and/or secondary public offering will provide the date the company first issued stock to the public (3-70), the number of shares that were issued (210,000), the initial offering price ($13. 3/4), and the name of the primary underwriter (Mitchum, Jones & Templeton Inc. et al.), that is, the investment banker who acts as the intermediary between the corporation who wishes to sell its stock and the general investing public who wish to buy it. Usually the primary underwriter will form a selling syndicate with a group of other investment bankers who will purchase the issue of stock directly from the corporation and resell the stock to the public at a markup. It is not uncommon for the primary underwriter and/or the selling syndicate to make a market in the securities that they have brought public. When an over-the-counter dealer specializes in certain securities, he is said to be making a market in those securities. This means he is willing to buy or sell the security. Contacting the initial underwriter is a possible source of determining the status of the "questioned stock."

J.   CLOSING MARKET—NASDAQ, MARCH 31, 1977— 5¼–6¼

This information tells us that the stock of the company is traded on the over-the-counter market and reported on NASDAQ, that is, the National Association of Securities Dealers Automatic Quotation System. The last reporting date was March 31, 1977, at which time the stock traded at $5.25 bid, $6.25 offered or asked. The $1 difference between the bid and asked price is commonly known as the *spread*. The "bid price" is the price at which a broker/dealer is willing to buy a unit of trading in the stock, while the "asked price" is the price at which he is offering it for sale. The narrower the spread, the greater the trading volume.

K.   RANGE—1977 7¼–5¼

Trading activity during 1977 has produced a high *bid* price of $7.25 and a low *bid* price of $5.25.

L.   MERRILL LYNCH PFS NY 1-30-76 9 10 D PRUDENTIAL-AMER SEC PSDNA 3-29-76 12½ 13½ D

Both Merrill Lynch Pierce Fenner and Smith of New York

and Prudential American Securities of Pasadena have been "making a market" in this stock. On January 30, 1976, Merrill Lynch PFS was quoting the stock at $9.00 bid offered at $10.00 (asked). On March 29, 1976 Prudential-Amer Sec was quoting the stock at $12.50 bid, $13.50 asked. The letter D indicates that these quotes were reported by the National Daily Quotation Service commonly known as the "Pink Sheets."

THE NEWS MEDIA

Just as we learned about the life-styles of ancient Egypt through the hieroglyphics found in the tombs of the Pharaohs, so will future generations learn about the events that shaped our social structure through records kept by the news media.

Since financial transactions are such an integral part of our society, nearly all daily, weekly, and monthly news publications will report such activities. As with other specialized fields of interest, there are many publications dedicated exclusively to the realm of business and finance.

The news media can be a very useful and reliable source of information when investigating questioned stocks. Copies of past editions of these publications, usually on microfilm, will provide you with not only last week's issue of a certain publication, but also that of many decades ago.

Since many financial occurrences, such as bankruptcies, liquidations, mergers, and acquisitions, are usually required to be made public information, the news media serve as the vehicle for the announcement. Most major libraries will have a periodical section in which past and present issues of significant news publications can be easily found.

In addition to consulting the major daily news publication in your particular area, the following list will provide you with the name, frequency, and place of publication of several other financially oriented publications:

American Investor
    American Stock Exchange
    New York (monthly magazine)

Bank and Quotation Record
    New York (monthly magazine)

Barron's: National Business and Financial Weekly
    New York (weekly newspaper)

Business Week
    New York (weekly magazine)

Commercial and Financial Chronicle
    New York (semiweekly newspaper)

The Exchange
    New York Stock Exchange
    New York (monthly magazine)

The Financial Analyst's Journal
    New York (bimonthly magazine)

Finance
    New York (monthly magazine)

Financial Times
    London (daily newspaper)

Financial World
    New York (weekly magazine)

Forbes
    New York (semimonthly magazine)

Fortune
    New York (semimonthly magazine)

Fundscope
    California (monthly magazine)

Investment Dealers' Digest
    New York (weekly magazine)

Journal of Commerce
    New York (daily newspaper)

Media General Financial Weekly
    Richmond, Va. (weekly newspaper)

Money
    Chicago, Ill. (monthly magazine)

O-T-C Market Chronicle
    New York (biweekly newspaper)

*Official Summary of Security Transactions
and Holdings*
    SEC, Washington, D.C. (monthly magazine)

Statistical Bulletin
    SEC, Washington, D.C. (monthly magazine)

Wall Street Journal
New York (daily newspaper)

Wall Street Transcript
New York (weekly newspaper)

This is not by any means a complete list of financial-and/or security-oriented publications; many others are published.

OTHER SOURCES

A truly thorough investigative procedure leaves no stone unturned. Although the following reference publications deal more with the current status of securities, past issues can provide the user with additional information which may be useful in his or her search.

The first source to be introduced is the *Standard & Poor's Stock Guide*, published monthly with a special year-end edition.[4] This laboriously produced reference work contains all pertinent stock data and can be used with confidence (see Figure 4-2).

The following explanations of the listings have been reproduced for your convenience through the courtesy of Standard & Poor's Corporation.

INDEX
The index numbers are a visual guide to the columnar data.

---

[4] Standard & Poor's Corporation, 345 Hudson Street, New York, NY 10014.

STOCK GUIDE

OCTOBER • 1977

Published

Note – Delivery date approximately October 20, 1977. Data revised through September 30, 1977. Delivery date of next issue about November 18, 1977.

UNIFORM FOOTNOTE EXPLANATIONS

Any statistical reference book requires numerous footnotes. To provide for consistency, eliminate repetition, and provide space to emphasize important individual situations requiring further explanation, the items recurring most frequently in the Stock Guide have been designated with specific symbols, the explanation of which will only appear on this page. Additional explanatory notations required appear at the bottom of respective pages.

EARNINGS PER SHARE are in general on a 'Primary' basis as reported by company, excluding extraordinary items. If common equivalents are dilutive, the primary earnings are prefixed by symbol ∫ : if potential dilution is significant, the extent is indicated for the latest year by reporting the "Fully Diluted" in the footnotes. Net operating earnings are shown for *banks*, earnings before appropriation to general reserve for *saving & loan associations*; net asset value for *mutual funds*; *railroads* as reported to ICC. *Foreign* issues traded ADR are in dollars, converted at prevailing exchange rate. Specific footnotes used in earnings columns:

* – Interim not comparable with annual earnings
§ – Net asset value
△ – Excludes extraordinary income
▲ – Includes extraordinary income
□ – Excludes extraordinary charge
■ – Includes extraordinary charge
∫ – Primary earnings (includes dilutive common equivalents)
• – Before tax loss carryforward
∧ – Comparison 1975 vs 1976

⊛ – Fully diluted earnings
‖ – Partial year
b – Before depletion
c – Company only
d – Deficit
E – S & P estimate
f – Net investment income
k – Currency of country of origin
N – Net gain from operations
p – Pro forma reflecting acquisitions, mergers, etc
P – Preliminary

LAST 12 MOS. indicates earnings computed through period shown in interim earnings column, unless otherwise footnoted. Where no interim period has been reported, last annual is given.

P-E RATIO Ratio is derived by dividing current price by estimated new year earnings or last 12 months earnings if no estimate is available.

INSTITUTIONAL HOLDINGS – Figures in these columns show how many financial institutions hold the stock in question, and how many shares (000 omitted) are so held. These data cover almost 2,400 institutions, including investment companies, banks, fire, casualty and life insurance companies, obtained from gathering sources. Not included are holdings of pension funds.

DIVIDENDS frequently include extra cash payments, stock, capital gains, payments on arrears, or may be before deduction of foreign income taxes. These and other situations dictate the use of uniform footnotes, as follows:

⊙ – Previous record (if any) not available
⊛ – Dividend from capital gains
⊛ – Excludes circled c type
↕ – Includes extras and stock
‡ – Div. paid in Canadian funds
‡ – Includes extras
a – Dividend paid a/c arrears
e – Excluding extras
g – In Canadian funds, less 15% or 10% non-residence tax depending on % Canadian ownership
h – Stock of another company

p – Pro forma reflecting acquisitions, mergers, etc
s – Also stock
t – Less tax country of origin
y – Based on last year's payment

OTHERS used in various columns:
‡ – Combined various classes
* – Giving effect to new financing
p – Pro forma reflecting acquisitions, mergers, etc
v – Non voting

STOCK SPLITS & DIVIDENDS are indicated by ♦ in the "Index" column, preceding the Dividend data. Details appear in footnotes which carry numerical symbols corresponding to those in the "Index" column. Adjustments of price ranges, dividends paid, and earnings have been made for all stock splits and stock dividends.

TABLE OF CONTENTS

How to use................Inside Covers
Stocks for Potential Appreciation and Income................Page 2
Selected Features................Page 3
Earnings and Dividend Rankings for Stocks................Page 4
Name Changes; New Insertions; Exchange Listings................Page 5

Abbreviations; Exchanges................Page 6
Standard & Poor's Composite Index of 500 Stocks................Page 7
Statistical Section................Pages 8–243
Quality Rankings of Utility Preferreds................Page 244
Mutual Funds—Summary................Pages 245–256

STANDARD & POOR'S CORPORATION, Publishers, 345 Hudson St., New York, N.Y. 10014
European Office: Standard & Poor's International, 45 boulevard Bischoffsheim, 1000 Brussels, Belgium
New York Stock Exchange and American Stock Exchange Monthly Volume, High-Low and Last Sale By The Associated Press

Figure 4-2   Sample pages from *Standard & Poor's Stock Guide*.

I N D E X	Some Divs. Ex. Yr. Since	DIVIDENDS						FINANCIAL POSITION				CAPITALIZATION			E n d	$ Per Shr—EARNINGS—$ Per Shr						INTERIM EARNINGS OR REMARKS			I N D E X
		Latest Payment			$ So Far 1977	Total Ind. Rate	$ Paid 1976	Cash& Equiv.	Mil-$ Curr. Assets	Curr. Liabs.	Balance Sheet Date	Long Term Debt Mil-$	Shs. 000 Pfd.	Com.		1973	1974	Years 1975	1976	1977	Last 12 Mos.	Period	S—Per Share—$ 1976	1977	
		P ?	$	Date	Ex. Div.																				
1♦	1945	Q0.15		9-9-77	8-16	0.41	d0.60	t0.290	1.72	28.2	23.2	6-30-77	5.66		1606	Dc	d0.07	0.30	1.40	2.62		2.48	12 Mo Jun	•2.11	△2.48	1
2	.....	None Since Public					Nil	....	1.41	5.23	3.99	5-31-77	6.17		4395	My	0.02	0.06	•0.44	0.39	0.22	0.22				2
3	.....	0.07		7-1-75	6-12		Nil	....	2.97	29.9	21.6	4-30-77	12.5		2178	Jl	1.09	0.75	d0.11	0.08		Nil	9 Mo Apr	0.14	0.06	3
4	1946	Q0.37½		9-15-77	8-26	1.12½	1.75	t1.65	37.4	90.4	20.2	6-30-77			13380	Dc	2.20	1.63	1.94	2.47	E2.70	2.47	6 Mo Jun	1.24	1.24	4
5	.....	None Since Public					Nil	....	0.31	4.76	1.17	7-3-77	1.13		1356	Mr	0.23	0.32	0.48	0.16		0.22	3 Mo Jun	0.02	0.08	5
6♦	1974	Q0.10		11-9-77	10-13	0.39	0.40	t0.437	2.23	66.5	19.4	7-30-77	35.8		2165	Dc	3.27	1.81	2.58	2.90		1.61	9 Mo Jul	2.48	1.19	6
7♦	1967	3%Stk		10-24-77	9-14	s0.963	1.00	0.895	155.	433.	187.	6-30-77	39.0		18553	Dc	1.44	3.24	5.19	4.87	E4.37	4.37	6 Mo Jun	2.39	1.89	7
8♦	1946	Q0.25		8-31-77	8-10	0.67	1.00	0.753	5.91	52.9	19.5	5-31-77	4.76		3013	Au	1.94	1.61	1.19	2.88		2.63	9 Mo May	2.22	1.97	8
9♦	1929	Q0.10		9-1-77	9-20	t0.40	0.41	t0.32	1.77	115.	44.6	6-30-77	36.3	3	‡11301	Ms	1.19	1.27	1.11	1.11		1.23	9 Mo Aug	0.67	0.79	9
10		Terms&trad.basis should be checked in detail							Pur Rapid-American common						472	Rate of $45.00 per full share							Warrants expire 3-15-81			10
11♦	1955	5%Stk		11-17-75	7-9-24		Nil	....	8.12	52.9	53.1	6-30-77	122.		17421	Dc	△0.14	△0.29	△0.16	d2.96		d2.98	6 Mo Jun	0.19	•0.17	11
12♦	1955	Q0.40		10-7-77	9-12	1.45	1.60	0.95	512.	912.	391.	6-30-77	165		15743	Mr	□2.50	4.93	•9.94	•33↑12.22	E8.00	12.75	12 Mo Jun	11.23	12.75	12
13	1976	Q0.05		11-15-77	10-18	0.17½	0.20	0.07½	99.2	166.	159.	6-30-77	529.		40514	Dc	1.31	1.64	2.17	2.72	E3.35	3.01	6 Mo Jun	1.30	1.59	13
14	1950	Q0.12½		10-3-77	8-30	0.48½	0.50	0.43	42.7	1742	1124	6-30-77	81.5		36805	Dc	3.36	2.77	2.27	2.85	E3.00	2.92	6 Mo Jun	1.48	1.55	14
15♦	1965	Q0.25		10-1-77	9-9	0.95	1.00	0.75	n/a	120.	30.6	7-31-77	18.1		3935	Ja	2.37	2.70	3.40?	△↑3.63	E4.00	3.76	6 Mo Jul	1.73	1.86	15
16♦	1973	0.07½		8-31-77	8-17	0.17½	0.17½	0.05	0.66	33.1	28.7	6-30-77	7.49		1403	Dc	1.44	1.34	0.13	f1.32		1.68	6 Mo Jun	0.62	0.98	16
17	.....	None Since Public					Nil	....	2.20	3.67	1.16	6-30-77	1.82		4075	Dc	•0.06	•0.38	•0.46	•0.49		0.58	6 Mo Jun	•0.15	•0.24	17
18	1934	Q0.40		9-15-77	8-16	1.20	1.60	1.40	58.3	485.	116.	6-30-77	57.3		16367	Dc	2.16	1.06	2.32	3.47	E3.55	3.48	6 Mo Jun	1.84	1.85	18
19	1937	Q0.20		9-14-77	8-23	0.60	0.80	0.64	43.8	262.	144.	6-30-77	34.9	702	23929	Dc	□1.11	□1.22	1.35	1.64		1.87	12 Mo Jun	1.52	1.87	19
20	1966	Q0.30		10-1-77	9-12	1.20	1.20	1.20	Conv into 1.65 shrs common					702		Dc	31.13	34.01	37.21	50.90		....				20
21♦	1975	0.10		10-31-69	10-10		Nil	....	0.01	16.2	4.23	6-30-77	8.70		‡1394	Dc	t•0.38	td1.34	td4.51	d0.55		d0.54	6 Mo Jun	d0.27	d0.26	21
22	1975	Q0.25		9-1-77	8-9	g0.75	1.00	g1.00	54.0	34.8	24.5	j6-30-77	54.0		2434	Dc	△6.61	5.20	•5.46	•5.66		5.93	6 Mo Jun	•2.10	2.37	22
23♦	1935	Q0.25		8-15-77	7-26	0.72½	1.00	0.80	48.0	106.	78.8	6-30-77	3.61		3171	Dc	•1.03	•1.66	2.12	2.69		2.82	6 Mo Jun	1.29	1.42	23
24	.....	None Since Public					Nil	....	Equity per shr $2.83			5-31-77	56.6	20	3390	Fb	0.54	d1.75	3.68	•△0.27		0.75	6 Mo Aug	d0.14	•0.34	24
25♦	1952	Q0.14½		10-1-77	8-26	0.49	0.58	0.31½	1.17	57.9	47.1	6-30-77	31.7		5622	Ja	1.83	2.07	1.79	2.68	2.73	2.73				25
26♦	1973	0.30		3-18-77	2-18	0.30	Nil	1.60	13.2	164.	104.	6-30-77	121.	55 10	5453	Dc	3.00	•3.89	1.07	2.03		1.65	6 Mo Jun	1.34	0.96	26
27	1976	S 0.05		6-30-77	6-1	0.10	0.10	•0.10	1.41	16.0	16.7	3-31-77	p30.3		*5848	Je	0.21	△0.04	0.22	•0.47	P0.43	0.43				27
28♦	1951	Q0.20		9-2-77	8-8	0.60	0.80	0.80	9.45	100.	36.6	6-30-77	22.0	2	3135	Dc	△2.02	△1.67	△1.11	△1.91	E1.75	2.19	6 Mo Jun	0.62	0.90	28
29♦	1956	Q0.30		9-26-77	9-6	0.56	0.80	0.60	3.56	62.7	22.1	6-30-77	22.0		2395	Dc	1.72	0.71	1.89	2.92		3.39	6 Mo Jun	1.59	2.06	29
30	.....	None Since Public					Nil	....	2.67	8.16	26.9	6-30-77	151.	321	20148	Mr	d1.59	d2.88	d1.66	d0.12		0.07	3 Mo Jun	△d0.18	•0.01	30
31	.....	None Paid					Nil	....	Equity per shr $5.74			5-31-77	7.57	17	716	Fb	•0.76	•*.28	•0.28	d2.03		d1.99	3 Mo May	•Nil	•0.04	31
32♦	1940	Q0.25		9-1-77	8-2	0.73	1.00	0.89	36.4	413.	223.	7-3-77	317.	p2267	22392	Dc	1.77	3.26	2.05	*3.61	E4.15	3.87	6 Mo Jun	1.71	1.97	32
33	1966	Q0.70		9-1-77	8-2	2.10	2.80	2.80	Ea1.15 Pfd Cv 3 sh com 2.61 sh				....p748			Dc	16.65	27.66	17.83	30.74		....				33
34	1969	Q0.70		9-1-77	8-2	2.10	2.80	2.80	Conv into 2.61 shrs common				....p1479			Dc	50	•3.33	•2.44	•3.22		....				34
35	1928	Q0.27		9-15-77	8-18	0.81	1.08	1.06	1.53	25.0	17.3	6-30-77			1663	Dc	1.61	1.86	1.92	1.61		1.70	6 Mo Jun	0.65	0.74	35
36	1977	Q0.08		11-18-77	10-21	0.08	0.32	....	9.27	68.9	26.0	5-31-77	44.2		3205	Nv	0.92	1.31	1.20	0.93	•....	1.52	9 Mo Aug	0.58	1.17	36
37	.....	None Since Public					Nil	....	2.98	1.08	1.07	6-30-77	0.22		1643	Dc	d0.03	d0.03	0.04	d1.11		0.20	6 Mo Jun	•0.07	•0.13	37
38♦	1966	Q0.11		10-15-77	9-26	0.41	0.44	0.372	1.52	52.5	21.1	6-30-77	18.4	15	1749	Dc	1.66	2.00	0.74	f1.15		1.35	6 Mo Jun	0.55	0.78	38
39	.....	0.05		1-16-67	12-27		Nil	....	0.82	21.4	19.0	6-30-77	13.7	133	2879	Dc	•0.15	0.10	d.15	0.10		0.15	6 Mo Jun	0.08	0.13	39
40	.....	None paid in cash					Nil	....	2.26	20.0	14.9	6-25-77	3.10		953	Mr	0.66	d0.12	0.25	■d4.23		d4.26	3 Mo Jun	d0.26	d0.29	40
41	.....	None Paid					Nil	....	1.34	6.23	1.50	6-30-77	0.42		1811	Dc	0.50	d0.48	0.13	d0.34		d0.29	6 Mo Jun	d0.01	d0.04	41
42	1972	Q0.07		9-30-77	9-9	0.19	0.28	0.14	2.10	19.2	13.1	6-30-77	27.4	4	1688	Dc	0.86	0.95	1.25	f1.52		1.81	6 Mo Jun	0.72	1.01	42
43♦	.....						Nil	....	2.24	4.61	2.59	3-31-77	6.95		893	Je	0.07	0.36	0.99	1.33	P1.62	1.62				43
44♦	1940	0.24		9-1-77	8-10	0.72	1.20	0.96	0.97	20.9	15.5	6-30-77	14.0		1223	Dc	5.01	1.23	2.15	2.26		3.03	6 Mo Jun	1.21	△1.98	44

◆ Stock Splits & Divs By Line Reference Index ¹10%,'77(ex '76). ⁹10%,'76,'77. ³2-for-1,'76;Adj to 3%,Sept'77. ⁴3-for-2,'76. ⁵2-for-1,'77. ¹¹Adj to 5%,'75. ¹²2-for-1,'75. ¹⁴5-for-4,'73. ¹⁸2-for-1,'73. ¹⁸10%,'73. ²⁸3-for-2,'73;2-for-1,'76. ²⁹2-for-1,'76. ³⁶3-for-2,'74. ⁴³3-for-2,'76. ⁴⁴3-for-2,'76. ⁴⁶@$0.97,'76;10%,'75,'77. ⁴⁷10%,'75,'76;Vote 10% stk,ex Oct 24. ⁴⁴5-for-4,'73. ⁴⁴⁵5-for-4,'77.

Figure 4-2 (Continued)

140 May-Med **STANDARD & POOR'S CORPORATION**

INDEX	Ticker Symbol	STOCKS NAME OF ISSUE (Call Price of Pfd. Stocks)	Market	Earns &Div Ranking	Par Val.	Inst. Hold Cos	Inst. Hold Shs. (000)	PRINCIPAL BUSINESS	PRICE RANGE 1960-75 High	1960-75 Low	1976 High	1976 Low	1977 High	1977 Low	Sep. Sales in 100s	September, 1977 Last Sale Or Bid High	Low	Last	% Div. Yield	P-E Ratio
1	MAYF	Mayflower Corp	OTC	NR	No	5	46	Moving/storage:transp eq	....	....	8½	6¼	8¾	7½	215	8¾	8½	8⅝B	e7.0	3
2	MOIL	Maynard Oil	OTC	B—	10¢	2	69	Oil/gas explor/dev:drill'g	4¾	1¼	4½	2⅝	4⅜	3¼	414	4⅛	3¼	4B	...	18
3	MJW	Mays, (J.W.)	NYS	B—	1	1	.8	Apparel dept stores,NY area	32½	2⅞	6⅜	2¾	3⅝	2¾	63	2⅞	2¾	2⅞	...	..
4	MYG	Maytag Co	NYS,Bo	A	2½	96	4229	Home laundry equipment	46¼	7¾	39	30¼	35⅞	28½	2758	31⅝	29	29⅜	†6.0	11
5	MBAS	MB Associates	OTC	B	1	..	...	Military govt systems	10⅜	⅞	3⅞	1⅝	2¾	1⅝	569	2⅝	2⅛	2⅝B	...	12
6	MXL	MBPXL Corp	NYS	NR	1	1	.2	Beef processor	26	4¾	14¼	8⅜	14¼	10	181	12¼	11	11⅜	3.5	7
7	MCA	MCA Inc	NYS,Ph,PS	B+	No	83	3863	TV film series: phono records	42	5⅜	39⅝	24¼	43	33	3983	38¼	33	33	s3.0	8
8	MCR	McCord Corp[51]	NYS,Ph	B+	3	13	235	Auto components: orig eqp	21	4¾	17¼	9½	30¾	15	10782	30¾	28⅛	30⅝	3.3	12
9	MCCRK	McCormick & Co[52]	OTC	A+	No	16	1801	Spices, flavoring, tea	33½	1 1/16	19⅞	16	19¼	15⅜	1820	18¼	15⅜	15¾B	†2.6	13
10	MS.WS	McCrory Wrrt(Pur½ com at$22.5)	ASE,PS	...	....	..	...	Merged into Rapid Amer'n	16¼	⅝	1⅝	¼	⅝	⅜	20	⅜	⅜	⅜	...	..
11	MCO	McCulloch Oil	ASE,Bo,Ph,PS	NR	50¢	11	108	Oil, gas, coal prod'n	34½	1⅛	5⅛	2½	4⅜	2⅞	2036	3⅜	3⅛	3¼	...	d
12	MDE	McDermott (J Ray)	NYS,Bo,Ci,MW,Ph	B+	1	136	5702	Offshore oil & gas constr	56¼	4¼	55¼	37⅞	59¾	43¼	5483	49¼	44¼	46⅜	3.5	6
13	MCD	McDonald's Corp	[1]NYS,Bo,Ci,MW,Ph,PS	A—	No	279	18591	Fast food restaurant:franch'g	77⅜	1⅛	66	48¾	53⅜	37¾	9814	50⅝	47¼	50	0.4	15
14	MD	McDonnell Douglas	NYS,Bo,Ci,Ph,PS	B	1	67	5192	Jet aircraft: space: missiles	45	2⅜	25	14¾	27¼	19⅜	4223	24½	20⅞	21⅜	2.3	7
15	MDO	McDonough Co	NYS	B+	1	7	269	Footwear, hand tools:cement	25¼	5⅞	21⅝	13¾	23¼	18¼	289	23¼	20½	21⅝	4.6	5
16	MCDL	McDowell Enterprises	OTC	B	No	2	23	Highway constrn: RE develop	14½	6	9¾	5⅞	11⅛	6⅛	631	11⅛	9¼	11⅛B	1.6	7
17	MCFE	McFarland Energy	OTC	NR	No	..	...	Oil & gas expl & prod'r	5	1⅝	3¾	1⅞	4½	2⅞	704	3⅜	3⅛	3¼B	...	6
18	MGR	McGraw-Edison	NYS,Bo,Ci,Ph	B+	1	62	2797	Electric eq:util,appl,ind'l	46¼	11⅛	32⅞	21¾	33	26⅛	1028	28	26¾	27¾	5.8	8
19	MHP	McGraw-Hill	NYS,Bo,MW,Ph,PS	★	1	92	7388	Books, film, instr svs: magaz	56½	5⅜	17⅛	12¾	20	15⅝	3345	19½	18	18⅞	4.2	10
20	Pr	$1.20 cm Cv Pref (40)vtg	NYS	★	10	7	18	& news letters: info sv,TV	91¾	12¾	28	20¾	32	26½	22	31	29¼	30½	3.9	..
21	MCGDA	McGregor-Doniger	OTC	C	1	2	33	Large mfr men's sportswear	15½	1	3	1⅛	1¾	1⅛	43	1⅜	1¼	1¼B	...	d
22	MP	McIntyre Mines	NYS([10]),MS,Ph,PS,TS	...	No	27	126	Falconbridge inv: coal mining	179½	18	48½	26⅛	37¾	25½	26	29½	25½	26⅜	3.8	4
23	MKE	McKee Corp	NYS,MW	B	No	8	373	Engr/constr for basic indust	17¾	3⅛	20⅞	10 1/16	20⅛	15⅛	271	17⅜	16⅛	16⅞	5.9	6
24	MKN	McKeon Construction	ASE,PS	NR	1	2	18	Homeowner apartments	40	1	4¾	1¼	5	3	151	3⅝	3⅛	3⅛B	...	4
25	MLN	McLean Trucking	NYS	A—	50¢	38	2299	Mtr freight common carrier	28 3/16	1 7/16	28⅜	18¼	26¼	18⅛	819	19	18⅜	18¾	3.1	7
26	MLX	McLouth Steel	NYS,Ph	B	2½	11	293	Flat rolled steel, mainly auto	41⅞	7⅜	23¾	16¾	18½	10⅝	811	12¼	10⅝	10¾	...	7
27	MMRN	McMoRan Exploration	OTC	NR	No	4	125	Oil & gas,U.S. & Canada	9⅞	1¼	13⅛	5⅜	17⅛	10¾	3498	13½	11¾	11¾B	0.9	27
28	MME	McNeil Corp	NYS	B+	No	7	459	Tire curing presses:lub:eq	30¼	6⅞	12½	9⅛	12⅝	10⅞	215	12¼	11¾	12	6.7	7
29	MCQA	McQuay-Perfex	OTC	B+	1	4	112	Air cond'g: refrig, heating eq	27⅛	3⅛	17¾	7	18½	13¾	475	18¼	16¾	17½B	4.6	5
30	MCIC	MCI Communications	OTC	NR	10¢	9	646	Microwave communic network	12⅛	⅞	3⅜	1⅜	3⅛	1¾	5220	3	2⅜	2⅜B	...	34
31	MNY	MDC Corp	ASE,Ph	NR	50¢	1	26	Leasing, finance, services	41	⅞	2⅞	1⅜	2⅛	⅞	419	2⅛	1⅜	1½	...	d
32	MEA	Mead Corp	NYS,Bo,Ci,MW,PS	B+	No	82	6910	Producer of white papers	22⅜	7⅜	23	12	24	18⅛	4537	21	18⅛	19½	5.1	5
33	Pr A	$2.80 cm Cv Pfd (60⅜)vtg	NYS,MW,PS	BBB	No	6	33	paperboards: furniture:	65	27½	59	35¾	61	49¼	69	55¾	53½	53½	5.2	..
34	Pr B	$2.80 cm Cv Pfd([59]60⅜)vtg	NYS,MW,PS	BBB	No	19	286	pipe & fittings,castings	66½	26	59½	36¾	61	49¾	44	55½	53½	53½	5.2	..
35	MNS	Means (F W) & Co	ASE,MW	B+	No	1	1	Full-line linen supplier	28¼	8¼	13½	10½	14¾	12¼	210	13¾	12¼	13½	8.0	8
36	MX	Measurex Corp	NYS,PS	NR	No	15	605	Ind'l process control sys	40⅜	9⅞	17½	8½	19⅜	10½	1328	18⅞	17¼	18⅞	1.7	12
37	MGNL	Med General	OTC	NR	1¢	..	...	Makes medical/surgical eq	2⅞	⅜	4⅝	1¾	7⅜	3	470	7⅜	6⅜	6⅝B	...	33
38	MDI	Medalist Indus	ASE	B+	1	1	3	Industrial & athletic products	21¾	3¾	8⅝	5⅛	8⅝	6½	244	8⅝	7⅛	7½	5.9	6
39	MGX	Medallion Group	ASE	C	1	..	...	Health-Chem sub: leisure prd	22¾	½	3⅜	1	2⅞	1½	557	2⅞	2¼	2¼B	...	15
40	MEO	Medco Jewelry	ASE	C	10¢	..	...	Jewelry depts in discount strs	25	1	4⅜	1¾	3½	1½	69	2⅞	2⅜	2⅜B	...	d
41	MEDC	Medcom, Inc	OTC	C	10¢	3	117	Health, medic info programs	28	1	3⅝	⅞	1⅝	⅝	142	1	¾	⅞B	...	d
42	MDX	Medenco, Inc	ASE	B+	1¢	5	103	Gen'l hospitals,dental labs	41½	2¾	9⅜	5⅞	13½	8⅛	1328	13½	11	13⅜	2.1	7
43	MED	Medfield Corp	ASE,Bo,PS	NR	40¢	..	...	Hospital mgmt & developm't	4⅛	1⅛	7⅞	1⅞	10½	5¼	538	10½	7⅞	10¼	...	6
44	MFRD	Medford Corp	OTC	B+	1	4	114	Building prods,mfd wood pr	36⅞	16	35¼	22⅞	37¼	31¼	111	35¼	35	35B	3.4	12

Uniform Footnote Explanations—See Page 1. Other: [1]TS. [51]Ex-Cell-O plans merger,option $31 cash or stk. [52]Non-vtg. [53]®$11.84,'77. [54]△$0.52,'76. [55]Pfd in Mil$. [56]$0.05,'76 non-taxable. [57]®$0.46,'76. [58]®$2.94,'76. [59]To 1978 only if com sells at $37.50 or over. [60]F.C.& Pfd Divds,Times Earned. [61]®$0.13,'76.
★S&P is a sub. of McGraw-Hill; common not ranked, pfd not rated.

Figure 4-2 (Continued)

TICKER SYMBOL

Ticker symbols on listed issues are those of the exchange first listed in the "Market" column. OTC (over-the-counter) stocks carry NASDAQ Trading System symbols. Supplementary symbols, i.e. those appearing on the ticker tape after the symbol (such as "Pr" for preferred stocks), are indented.

STOCKS, NAME OF ISSUE (CALL PRICE OF PFD. STOCKS) MARKET

Names shown in this column are not necessarily the exact corporate title of the company. Also, because of space limitations, the occasional use of abbreviations has been necessary. Where the name of the company is not followed by the designation of any particular issue of its stock, it is the common or capital stock that is referred to.

The call price of preferred stocks is shown in parentheses after the name of the issue; the date indicates year in which call price declines. Abbreviations of various provisions, etc., are shown on page 84.

The unit of trading for stocks on the New York Stock Exchange and American Stock Exchange is indicated as follows:

10-10 shares; 25-25 shares; 50-50 shares; all others 100 shares.

The markets for each issue are indicated by standard abbreviations, as shown on page 84. Stocks traded "over the counter" are indicated by the abbreviation OTC; it will be noted that some issues may have an active OTC market as well as exchange markets.

EARNS & DIV. RANKING
Standard & Poor's ranking system is explained on page 83.

PAR VAL.
Present par value of the stock named. In determining transfer taxes, no par issues are figured the same as $100 par.

INST. HOLD, COS—SHS. (1000)
The number of financial institutions—banks, investment and insurance companies—that hold this stock and the number of shares held.

PRINCIPAL BUSINESS
This is the principal business of the company. Where a company is engaged in several lines of business, every effort has been made to list that line from which it obtains the greatest proportion of its revenue. In addition, an indication of the company's rank in the industry is given where possible.

PRICE RANGE, HISTORICAL/LAST YEAR/CURRENT YEAR (HIGH/LOW)
High and low price ranges are for the calendar years indicated.

Price ranges are not exclusive for the exchange on which the stock is currently traded, but are based on the best available data covering the period of the column head. Price ranges of over-the-counter stocks are based on the best available high and low bid prices during the period, and should be viewed as reasonable approximations.

MONTH SALES IN 100s
Trading volume is for the month indicated on the composite tape, in hundreds of shares.

LAST MONTH OTC—BID PRICES (HIGH/LOW/LAST)
Last sales on principal exchanges are closing quotations for the preceding month. In the case of Canadian issues, prices are quoted in Canadian dollars providing the first exchange listed is a Canadian exchange.

In the case of over-the-counter stocks, the latest available bid price is shown under the "Last" column.

% DIV. YIELD
Yields are derived by dividing total indicated dividend rate by price of stock. Such rate is based on latest dividend paid, including (+) or excluding (e) extras as indicated by the footnote. Additional symbols used: (s) including stock, and ($^{+}_{+}$) including extras and stock.

P-E RATIO
P-E (price-earnings) ratio—See explanation on page 80.

SOME DIV. EA. YR. SINCE
One or more cash dividends have been paid each year to date, without interruption, beginning with year listed.

LATEST PAYMENT, PER $/DATE/EX. DIV.
Per $: Latest dividend payment. If at a regular established rate, it is so noted by M (monthly), Q (quarterly), S (semi-annually), or A (annually).

Date: Date of disbursement of the latest payment. If an extra or stock dividend also is being paid, it is so indicated by footnote.

Ex. Div.: The date shown is that on which the stock sells "ex-dividend," that is, the date on which it sells without the right to receive the latest declared dividend.

TOTAL, THIS YEAR/IND. RATE/LAST YEAR

This year: Payments made or declared payable thus far in the current calendar year, including both regular and extras, if any.

Ind. Rate: S&P projection of dividend payments for next 12 months, used to compute percentage dividend yield.

Last Year: Total dividend payments, including extras if any, made in the preceding calendar year. For preferred dividend accumulations to latest payment due date, see 'Financial Position" or "Remarks" column.

FINANCIAL POSITION, CASH & EQUIV./CURR. LIABS., BALANCE SHEET DATE

Cash & Curr. Equiv. Assets: Cash & equivalent, current assets, and current liabilities are given in millions of dollars (000,000 omitted); for example, 17.0 = $17,000,000, 1.75 = $1,750,000, 0.18 = $175,000.

Curr. Liabs., Balance Sheet Date: Where current balance sheet items are not of analytical significance, special calculations pertinent to the industry in which the company operates are presented, as "book value per share" for banks and finance companies, "net asset value per share" for investment trusts, and "equity per share" (stockholders) for insurance companies.

CAPITALIZATION, LONG-TERM SHS. 000, MIL $/PFD./COM.

Long-term debt is in millions of dollars; for example, 25.0 = $25,000,000, 2.58 = $2,580,000, 0.20 = $200,000. It includes funded debt, long-term bank loans, mortgages, etc. Preferred and common stocks are in shares to the nearest thousand (000 omitted); for example, 150 = 150,000 and 30 = 30,000. Outstanding shares exclude treasury stock. Figure shown under preferred shares column on company name line represents the combined number of preferred shares outstanding.

ANNUAL EARNINGS, PER SHARE, LATEST FIVE YEARS/LAST 12 MOS.

Earnings are in general on a "primary" basis as reported by the company, excluding extraordinary items. More detailed information on method of reporting and usage of standard footnotes can be found on page 80.

Earnings for fiscal years ending March 31 or earlier are shown under the column of the preceding calendar year.

S&P earnings estimates are the final product of careful analysis by industry specialists of available relevant information. They are unofficial, however, and responsibility for their accuracy cannot be assumed.

Last 12 Months indicates 12 months' earnings through

the period shown in the interim earnings column, when available, or annual, if not.

INTERIM EARNINGS OR REMARKS: PERIOD/$ PER SHARE COMPARISON

Interim earnings are shown, when available, for the longest accounting interval since the last fiscal year-end. Also published in this column from time to time are references to exchanges of shares, mergers, name changes, etc. See also Financial Position column for such notations.

INDEX

The index numbers are a visual guide to the columnar data.

In addition to the *Stock Guide*, other useful Standard & Poor's Corporation publications include:

Corporation Records
A loose-leaf service kept up-to-date by a separate Daily News Section.

Dividend Record
Up-to-date information on corporation dividends. Cumulated annually.

Earnings Forecaster
Published weekly; devoted to providing the financial community with a current report of earnings estimates by leading investment organizations.

Industry Surveys
Analyses of principal industries, including trends and forecasts.

Security Dealers of North America
> Directory of all the investment firms in the United States and Canada.

Stock Reports
> Loose-leaf volumes which include basic information on all stocks on the American, New York, Over-the-Counter, and Regional Exchanges. Frequently revised.

The Investment Statistics Laboratory (ISL), a division of Standard & Poor's, 345 Hudson Street, New York, publishes the following:

ISL Daily Stock Price Index: American Stock Exchange

ISL Daily Stock Price Index: New York Stock Exchange

ISL Daily Stock Price Index: Over-the-Counter and Regional Exchanges

Provided on a quarterly basis, this useful and time-saving service contains a section devoted to the market indicators used most frequently as well as a section giving the daily and weekly record of all stocks listed on each of the exchanges.

Among other sources of information which can be found in the business section of the public library are:

Moody's Investors Service, Inc., 99 Church Street, New York:

*Moody's Manuals of Investment, American &
Foreign*
Annual volumes covering the fields of Banks and
Finance; Industrials; Municipals and Government;
OTC Industrials; Public Utilities; Transportation.
Kept up to date with semiweekly news bulletins.

Arnold Bernhard & Co., Inc., 5 East 44th Street,
New York:
The Value Line Investment Survey
A weekly advisory service which reports on busi-
ness conditions as well as economic changes.
Makes specific recommendations.

Wiesenberger Financial Services, 5 Hanover Square,
New York:
Investment Companies
An exhaustive compendium issued annually. Includes data on the background and management
policy as well as income, dividends, and price
ranges for each listing.

When investigating obsolete securities it is extremely
important to establish a time reference. Keeping in mind
that these sources contain current information on active
securities, their usefulness, when dealing with questioned
stocks, is in past issues, which can possibly be obtained
directly from these companies.

After carrying out your investigation using the methods
set forth in these two chapters, you will be able to draw a

final conclusion. In the event it is determined that your particular questioned stock is defunct or otherwise valueless, you can use this information to your advantage. Depending upon your own financial situation, a tax benefit may be realized. Because of the varying nature of tax laws and differing individual financial positions, it is suggested that a tax adviser or accountant be consulted.

Quite frequently the investigative effort will be rewarded with a valuable find. The magnitude of such gains will differ depending upon each individual circumstance, and the transference of securities may be necessary. This can be accomplished through various channels, which include transfer agents, stockbrokers, and in some cases the company itself. There may be tax considerations, and again we suggest professional advice.

In any event, positive results will have been obtained in determining the status of your questioned stock.

CHAPTER FIVE

SAVE THAT PRETTY WALLPAPER: STOCK AND BOND CERTIFICATES AS COLLECTIBLES*

THE MINING SECURITIES

It was only three days before expiration of conversion privileges of a certain mining company's securities when R. M. Smythe & Company received the name of a woman who was entitled to $24,000 for her shares. Unless the woman was found and tendered her securities, all would be lost.

---

* The authors wish to express their gratitude to John and Diana Herzog and to Robert Fisher, Jr., for all their invaluable assistance.

Given enough time and interest, almost anyone can be found, but in this particular instance, it was a race *against* time. The only scrap of evidence that Smythe had to work with was a similar name of a person living in California, hopefully a relative. Smythe quickly contacted this person and discovered that the woman they were seeking was now residing in Maine.

Since time was of the essence, the Smythe firm began preparing all documents necessary for the conversion. When the woman was finally reached at her home by telephone, she was informed of the situation and told that a representative of R. M. Smythe was on his way.

The conversion was completed, and the woman received the funds due her—with just hours to spare.[1]

> *In January 1978, a woman living in California discovered two stock certificates among her late husband's estate papers. The 150 shares of Southern and Atlantic Telegraph Company, dated in the mid 1940s, were not being quoted and were therefore assumed to be worthless.*
>
> *Through the efforts of R. M. Smythe & Company, it was ascertained that the Southern and Atlantic Telegraph Company had been incorporated in 1868 and acquired by the Western Union Telegraph Company in 1958. More important, the stock was still convertible at $19.72 per share. The woman's payment came to nearly $3000!*

JOHN HERZOG
PRESIDENT, R. M. SMYTHE & CO.

---

[1] John Herzog.

R. M. Smythe & Company was founded in 1880 by Roland M. Smythe, a stockbroker who had acquired a consuming interest in obscure securities. He began to accumulate information on stocks and bonds going back to 1832; he also cultivated the presidents of railroads, banks, and utilities in order to learn about contemporary developments as they came along—and carefully catalogued the data he acquired.

These pioneering efforts became the foundation of R. M. Smythe & Company, Inc., specialists in evaluation of obscure and unusual securities. The company's considerable publishing efforts began in 1904, when Smythe published *Obscure American Securities and Corporations*—still a fascinating and authoritative book.

Meanwhile, the Robert D. Fisher Service, publisher of the *Fisher Manuals of Valuable and Worthless Securities*, was founded in 1926 to perform a similar service for investors. Fourteen manuals have been published in this series, the latest in 1975.

In 1967, the Fisher Service was acquired by R. M. Smythe & Company, and the combined resources of the two firms thereby came to include a special library of over 3000 volumes and unique files on well over a million securities. Today R. M. Smythe, with excellent research facilities, provides a valuation service covering corporations throughout the world.

"The old stock certificate, as we know it, is probably on its last leg," states John Herzog, president of R. M. Smythe & Company, "and there is an increasing indication that people are collecting those that are left." The Smythe firm receives many inquiries from collectors and dealers, since part of their business is the buying and selling of old certificates.

The attitude of many certificate collectors has changed, perhaps inspired by the recent Bicentennial celebration, from collecting certificates for casual decoration to an increasing awareness of our country's historical development as told through old securities.

Such historic figures as Paul Revere, who himself was a fine engraver as well as a staunch patriot, have left behind beautiful examples of colonial-era documents. Many Revolutionary War fund-raising bonds were not only masterpieces of engraving but also bear the signatures of some of the greatest men of their time—many of whom were signers of the Declaration of Independence or delegates to the Constitutional Convention. These rare documents have a tremendous historical value, and in certain cases, although they can no longer be redeemed, they are worth many times their original face value to collectors.

In the eighteenth and early nineteenth centuries, the method of creating cultural establishments such as churches, libraries, museums, art galleries, and music centers was through the issuance of "shares"; the Brooklyn Academy of Music is one such example.

Various state and local securities issued during the nineteenth century are often signed by officials who later rose to fame and prominence in our political system. There is an issue of New York State guaranteed stock signed by the then comptroller, Millard Fillmore, who later became the twelfth president of the United States. An interesting but not well-known fact is that George McClellan, a famous Civil War general, later went on to become president of the Atlantic and Great Western Railway Company, with his signature appearing on those certificates. Many political figures throughout our history, either prior to or after their administrations, had affiliations with commercial enterprises, and their signatures on old certificates have made them prized collector's items.

The dramatic development of American industry in the late nineteenth and early twentieth century brought many more people to fame and fortune. This was the age of the "robber barons," and such famous names as Rockefeller, Carnegie, Vanderbilt, Sage, Livermore, Mellon, and Morgan, to name a few, appear on the certificates of their respective companies; although many are intrinsically worthless, they command a good price for these famous signatures.

A good suggestion when looking for signatures would be to examine the back of the certificate as well as the front. Like a check or bank draft, a stock certificate must be endorsed on the back to be "cashed" or sold. Certificates owned by famous people may carry their signature on the back, and although canceled, the certificate may have value for the autograph. One very ironic example of this is provided by two complementary certificates of the Pennsylvania Population Company dated 1795—one signed on the back by Aaron Burr, the other by Alexander Hamilton.

Some of the earlier securities issued (mostly bonds) were not only payable (principal and interest) in U.S. currency and specie but also in a variety of "hard" commodities, such as bushels of corn, pounds of beef, sheep's wool, salt, etc. These issues give us a valuable insight into the economics of the day; the inflation we are battling at present is not a new problem in our country.

"Another value arises in the sheer beauty of the printed paper, and that can be very meaningful," says John Herzog. Ringling Bros., Barnum & Bailey Circus stock, when acquired by Mattel, the toymaker, did not yield all the shares tendered for. Many holders kept one or two share certificates as a memento mainly because the unique pictorial circus scenes on the document. These original certificates will probably never be seen again.

However, ". . . there are always items turning up which are very interesting both financially and historically. You never know when you're going to find one. People have these things and are not aware of their value. They think of them as curios, when, in fact, they have become quite valuable." The early automobile stocks of the 1920s are very highly prized by collectors. There are only a handful of auto manufacturers left in the United States today, but at the time there were a score or more. To say that they are very highly prized does not make *all* of them very valuable, but they should be investigated before being discarded. There are a great many shares of securities locked away that have substantial values—not only as collectibles, but also for possible redemption. Confederate bonds issued to help finance the South's effort in the Civil War do not have any liquidating value, but they certainly are very important collector's items.

Are we saying, then, that old securities are collectibles

similar to coins, stamps, or art? "Yes—very definitely," states Herzog, "and as with coins and stamps, condition and date play a big role in their value, as do many other factors, such as the quantity available." However, some documents, although not in the best condition, have a character all their own. An old Russian war bond in Mr. Herzog's collection, which has been repaired several times, shows the traumas that it went through over the years and has a certain charisma that it would not possess if in mint condition. Some securities have survived two or more major wars, economic strife, transportation to different continents, and the like, and they show the scars of the experience.

These certificates can also be classified as antiques, not only for their beauty of engraving, which represents an era coming inevitably to an end, but also for their historic and financial value. Collectors of these certificates are growing in number rapidly, and for a very good reason: "I think it's very good for the country to preserve as much of this material as possible," says Herzog. "This is one way of getting a much clearer understanding of where the country has been." And maybe of where it is going.

CHAPTER SIX

DETECTION AND RECOGNITION OF FRAUDULENT SECURITIES*

The phrase "not worth the paper it's printed on" applies as much to some stock certificates as to many other documents of dubious value. Shares of stock, whether of the largest corporation in the world or the smallest, are absolutely worthless if not authentic. Today's technology has made great strides in lessening the chance of stock certificates being counterfeit, but the possibility is not totally eliminated:

---

* The authors are very grateful to the American Bank Note Company for allowing us to use their materials in connection with this chapter.

It's preposterous, but a Miami bank once gave a woman a loan on 8,000 shares of Kayser-Roth stock that didn't bear even a faint resemblance to K-R stock. Says a spokesman for the American Bank Note Co.: "The forger had completely redrawn the certificate." The forgery was discovered only when a bank official started wondering how the woman had come into the stock. He had known her for years as a small depositor.

United States banks are not alone in being suckered by counterfeits. German banks have been flooded with them. Not long ago in Dusseldorf, the banks discovered they were holding $2.5 million worth of counterfeit American Telephone & Telegraph, Pan American World Airways, General Electric, and Chrysler securities. About the same time, a Zurich bank accepted over $2 million worth of securities in the same companies.

Once a counterfeit is discovered, the exchange sends a memorandum to brokers and bankers warning them about the counterfeit and detailing how it can be detected.[1]

Although this story is more the exception than the rule today, older issues of securities (which in many cases are inherited, found in attics, basements, antique shops, etc.) have a greater possibility of being counterfeit.

As stated in an earlier chapter, our society uses symbols or tokens of our rights, powers, and possessions. These symbols generally take the form of paper documents.

The successful use of such documents rests upon the confidence which can be placed in their validity. The cost of manufacturing a document of value is very small com-

---

[1] "Easy to Forge," *Forbes Magazine*, April 1, 1973, p. 27. Reprinted by permission.

pared with what it may represent, and its intrinsic value is practically nil. Yet every day, hundreds of millions of dollars are paid with confidence in exchange for these special pieces of paper.

If there ever should arise grounds for general doubt of the validity of documents of value, whether bank notes, stock certificates, bonds, traveler's checks, or stamps, the ensuing paralysis of economic life would be appalling. That is why a world which is divided on so many of its other beliefs agrees on the importance of maintaining confidence in documents of value. Throughout the world, stringent penalties are imposed on convicted counterfeiters. In a more forthright age, a century and a half ago, bank notes in English-speaking countries frequently bore the words: " 'Tis Death to Counterfeit," and statutes made the threat a real one. In the present-day United States, the Secret Service is a special government organization with two duties: (1) the prevention and detection of counterfeiting and (2) the protection of the President of the United States, members of his family, the President-elect, and the Vice President, at his request.

But the use of police power alone cannot prevent a serious amount of counterfeiting, even with death and torture as penalties. The evidence of history on this point is clear. A more important safeguard, therefore, is the principle that documents of value must be made so difficult to copy that to do so is unattractive to those undeterred by moral considerations or the threat of punishment.

The task of making documents that defy counterfeiters is the province of what is known as the bank note industry.

It is a small industry by comparison with many others, yet its products probably enter into the lives of more individual men and women throughout the world than do those of any other group.

SECURITY PRINTING

Security printing is different from most other activities in many respects, but chiefly in that its products represent values which are hundreds, even thousands, of times their cost. Caution, aloofness, and secrecy are therefore inescapable, as are many unusual business policies. For example, no customer, whether corporation or government, may obtain possession of the engravings from which its documents have been printed. As another example, all the important scientific advances of the last century and a half that have related to the graphic arts or visual reproduction have had to be considered first as potentially dangerous weapons in the hands of counterfeiters, and only then as possibly useful adjuncts to the industry. The invention of the camera, for instance, required prompt countermeasures, and the invention of film and filter combinations, by which a camera could select a single color and ignore others, demanded another change in strategy. There would be considerable truth in the statement that, while other industries direct their research to finding easier ways to make their products, the conscientious security printer seeks to find more difficult ways. There are no open-house nights in a money factory, and no free samples!

A more subtle difference is this: While the general tendency of industry is to eliminate the personal characteristics of individual craftsmen, bank-note engraving carefully continues them, even stresses them, because, despite all technological advances, the counterfeiter's most baffling problem is the unique personality of the artist which the engraving process transmits directly to the document.

Since no photography enters into its creation, an engraved document cannot be duplicated by it. (A camera can of course make a picture of an engraved document, but that is very different from duplicating it—a camera can make a picture of a cat, but it cannot make a kitten.) Therefore, another engraving would be necessary, which under comparative examination could not fail to reveal a personal touch different from the original.

Beyond defeating counterfeiters from the standpoint of expert examination of documents, every effort is put forth to make their spurious products apparent even to cursory or nonexpert examination. The most advanced achievements of the industry have been strikingly successful in both respects.

Security printing has its technicalities, which are an integral part of its history. A few terms and principles can be explained here.

THREE METHODS OF PRINTING

There are three fundamentally different ways to make printed impressions on paper. To see how they differ, we can imagine a man sitting at a table with sheets of paper, ink (not liquid, but thick like toothpaste), and a piece of some smooth washable material, say a piece of linoleum. He wants to print an "X" on each sheet of paper.

The man has three choices:

(1) He can mark an X on the linoleum with ink, then press each sheet of paper in turn against it, renewing the ink on his X as necessary. This is *surface printing*, of which the principal commercial example is lithography. In place of our amateur's linoleum, in this process the paper is pressed against a stone or rubber surface, depending upon whether it is direct or offset lithography.

(2) He may use a knife to cut down the entire surface of the linoleum except where his X is marked, so that the X stands higher than the material around it. When he runs an inked roller over his work, only the elevated X surface will be coated with the ink. A sheet pressed down on his work will touch the elevated surface only, and will be marked with the X. This was originally known as *cameo printing*, but it is more popularly called *letterpress*. It is the method of the traditional printing industry, and also of the woodcut and the humble rubber stamp. The material used is generally a lead alloy, zinc, or copper.

(3) He may, however, use his knife for a different purpose—to cut an X *into* the surface of the linoleum, the way he once carved initials into the surface of his school desk. Next he coats the linoleum with ink, then thoroughly wipes the ink from the level surface, leaving it only in the recessed cuts. When a sheet of paper is pressed down firmly on the linoleum and into the carved X, this ink will adhere to it

and be pulled out of the recess when the sheet is withdrawn, so that it remains as an X with appreciable thickness on the paper. This is *intaglio* printing. Typical examples include security printing, other forms of engraving such as that used for fine wedding announcements, and gravure, which is the photomechanical version of intaglio printing. The material used is steel, copper, or zinc.

STRINGENT REQUIREMENTS FOR VALUABLE DOCUMENTS

The stock certificates and bonds that are handled every working day are among the most valuable documents in the financial community. In order to minimize the possibility of counterfeiting and forgery, the New York Stock Exchange and other major exchanges have established extremely strict requirements as to how these documents are to be printed.

Stock certificates and bonds traded on these exchanges are printed by only a small number of bona fide bank note companies, all employing printing processes which produce a document that is unique in the financial world.

Among the requirements of these exchanges is the intaglio printing of major portions of the stock and bond certificates. The quality of the intaglio printing determines, to a great degree, the amount of protection the certificates will have.

Human figures are required in vignettes appearing on New York Stock Exchange–listed securities because human flesh tones and flowing robes afford the engraver the opportunity to develop light and dark areas, through the use of fine and heavy lines. Lithographic reproductions of genuine securities flatten out the lines, causing a muddied or mottled appearance or a washed-out, flat look.

The care and skill with which the engraving and printing are executed and the safeguards surrounding the production of a security document assure the best protection against alteration or duplication. Bank note companies continually strive to foil their enemy—the camera lens. The recent development of high-quality color xerographic equipment has added a new dimension to the threat of illegal duplication and fraud. Color xerography and other color duplicating systems could provide unscrupulous amateurs with a means of instant counterfeiting.

Security features combining special paper and inks, coupled with engravings, are tools used in various degrees by all bank note companies. The American Bank Note Company has developed a number of additional special techniques. The "intaglio latent image" (patented by the American Bank Note Company) is an example of a security feature which can be produced only by the intaglio printing process from engraved plates. The same company has also pioneered in the use of *planchettes*, small paper disks embedded in the surface of the paper used for securities. The planchettes always appear in securities carrying the imprint "American Bank Note Company" at the bottom of each certificate. These security features are discussed in detail on the following pages.

AIDS IN DETECTING COUNTERFEITS

The frequency with which counterfeit documents have appeared in recent years poses a direct threat to business and financial institutions, as well as to those who are share-owners of corporations. (Awareness of a fraudulent document can be achieved through a knowledge of what to look for.) Detection of counterfeits is not difficult.

On the following pages a table is provided which summarizes the more important distinctions which can be made between a genuine document and lithographic or xerographic reproductions. A checklist is also provided recommending a quick method for establishing the genuineness of certificates.

INTAGLIO PRINTING

The use of the intaglio process to print securities provides these documents with characteristics which are unique. Only by the intaglio printing of engraved subjects can the sharpness, clarity, and three-dimensional qualities exhibited by genuine documents be obtained. Either the border or the corporate title (and in many instances both) of a genuine certificate will always have a raised, coarse feel to the fingers. The surface of the paper containing the border and vignette is always smoother in appearance than the surface on the back, which is always slightly rough.

THE INTAGLIO LATENT IMAGE

The intaglio latent image is the result of years of research effort by the American Bank Note Company. The intaglio latent image provides a simple and effective means of document verification. Although not all genuine securities contain the latent image at the present time, its use in securities, as well as other intaglio-printed documents, is increasing.

The intaglio latent image is not visible under normal viewing conditions. The following description tells how to make it appear:

1. Hold the document up above eye level, positioned between the eyes and a ceiling light or window.

2. Tilt the top of the document back until the image appears in the appropriate area.

3. While observing the image, rotate the document to either side without changing the angle of the document. Notice how the image disappears and reappears either darker or lighter than observed in the original position.

Step (3) is very important and should never be eliminated whenever examining an intaglio latent image.

PLANCHETTES

Planchettes are small circles of special papers, about the size of the head of a straight pin, which are embedded into the surface of the paper. Although a genuine security will contain numerous planchettes on both the face and back of the document, only the following four colors are used by American Bank Note: (1) *pink*, which will shine or fluoresce red under an ultraviolet lamp (black light); (2) *yellow*, which will fluoresce yellow under an ultraviolet lamp; (3) *blue*, which contains strands of blue fibers; and (4) *orchid*, which contains strands of both red and blue fibers.

While these fibers may be difficult to see with the naked eye, they are readily visible when examined with an ordinary magnifying glass.

Although counterfeiters occasionally attempt a simulation of planchettes by printing small circles of color, they have never achieved the effect of the colored fibers in the blue and orchid planchettes.

The planchettes on genuine documents always appear in random positions. If many or all of the planchettes appear in exactly the same positions on two documents, the documents are suspect and should be examined thoroughly.

TABLE 6-1 IDENTIFYING COUNTERFEIT DOCUMENTS—(Continued)

Area of Document	Genuine	Litho Reproduction	Color Reproduction
Most distinguish-ing feature	Sharp, clear vignette.	Poor quality of vignette.	Poor quality of vignette. Secondary coloring.
Xerox rub test black corporate title	When rubbed with white paper, a black smudge is obtained.	When rubbed with white paper, a black smudge is obtained.	When rubbed with white paper, a blue-green smudge is usually obtained.
Intaglio latent image	Hidden when viewed face on. Ex-posed when held up and viewed obliquely.	Cannot be seen.	Cannot be seen.

TEN QUICK CHECKS FOR GENUINENESS

1. Is the vignette (or picture) sharply detailed black ink, with no secondary colors?

2. Does the corporate title and script or the border have a raised, coarse feel?

3. Is the border printed with crispness and clarity?

4. Are planchettes visible in four different colors?

5. Are the fibers in the blue and orchid planchettes visible under a glass?

6. Is the CUSIP number (on more recent issues of securities) flat with the surface of the paper?

7. Does the back surface of the paper look and feel rougher than the paper surface on the face of the document?

8. Are straight parallel lines, as in the Number and Shares panels, uniform in color and appearance?

9. Is the ink dull (not glossy)?

10. If the document contains an intaglio latent image, does the image appear when viewed properly (obliquely)?

If the answer to any of the above questions is no, it would be wise to examine the document further.

SIXTY YEARS OF CORPORATE UPS, DOWNS, AND OUTS (1917–1977)[1]

When *Forbes* published its first issue in September of 1917, many of the corporations that were to stand out in U.S. business over the subsequent sixty years were already well-established giants. U.S. Steel was the biggest industrial company at that time, with over $2 billion in assets. Also among the very largest companies were such familiar names as Standard Oil of New Jersey (now Exxon), International Harvester, du Pont, General Electric, Ford Motor.

---

[1] *Forbes Magazine*, Sept. 15, 1977. Reprinted by permission.

Critics of the U.S. economic system, Harvard professor John Kenneth Galbraith prominent among them, have charged that the modern corporation's great size has made a farce of the concept of competition—the big just get bigger at the expense of everybody else. But as the following pages show, the summit of U.S. corporate success is a slippery one, and sheer size is no guarantee of prosperity or even survival.

The tables show that a surprising number of the one hundred largest companies in the U.S. in 1917 have slipped badly. Armour and Swift, the meatpackers, were among the top *five* corporations in the U.S. in 1917; neither remains among the top one hundred companies today. Nor does American Smelting & Refining (now ASARCO), which was number twelve in 1917; or Anaconda Copper (thirteenth in 1917); Phelps Dodge (fifteenth); Singer Manufacturing (sixteenth); B. F. Goodrich (twenty-third); or Pullman (twenty-sixth in 1917).

On the other hand, you've probably at least *heard* of most of those companies. But have you ever heard of International Mercantile Marine? It was the eleventh largest company in the U.S. in 1917. How about Central Leather? It was twenty-fourth. Number thirty-eight was American Woolen, number fifty-eight was Atlantic Gulf & West Indies, number sixty-one was American Locomotive, number seventy-eight was Baldwin Locomotive, and number one hundred was a company called United Verde Extension Mining. Almost all of those companies have gone out of business, or nearly so. International Mercantile Marine is now known as U.S. Lines and is just a subsidiary of Walter Kidde & Company, which is having trouble disposing of it. American Woolen, which Royal Little, founder of Textron, took over to build his famous conglomerate, is only a memory.

Critics of the U.S. system would likely respond that they prefer to focus on the period following World War II—which to them represents the heyday of the corporate enterprise so high and mighty that it is virtually impervious to the forces of competition.

The contention doesn't hold much water. Look at our list of the hundred largest companies in 1945. Jersey Standard, U.S. Steel, du Pont, and General Electric were still near the top. They were joined in the top ten by some companies that had ranked in the low thirties back in 1917—General Motors, Texas Company (later Texaco), and Standard Oil of Indiana. All of these, of course, remain huge today.

Yet dozens of the top one hundred companies at the end of World War II are conspicuous by their *absence* from the 1977 list. Among them: Anaconda, thirteenth in 1945; Montgomery Ward, a proud twenty-seventh in 1945; Curtiss-Wright, which held the twenty-eighth spot. Also on the list of the top one hundred companies in 1945—and gone from the 1977 list—are Loew's Inc., Warner Brothers, Schenley Distillers, American Viscose, and United Shoe Machinery.

Several of these companies have fallen on hard times; some were absorbed by other companies. Once-mighty Anaconda was recently merged into Atlantic Richfield. Montgomery Ward was left in the dust by Sears, Roebuck and is now part of Mobil Corp. Schenley Distillers is part of Rapid-American Corp., controlled by wheeler-dealer Meshulam Riklis. What's left of American Viscose was lately spun off by owner FMC Corp.

All in all, sixty-five of the top one hundred in 1917, and forty of the top one hundred in 1945, are no longer on the list today. Some of the companies that replaced them came from virtually nowhere to the top in a matter of decades. Among them: Tenneco, Litton Industries, Xerox.

To some extent, the rise and fall of corporate giants can be ascribed to technology: locomotive and leather companies were obviously victims; computer companies and oil companies were right where the action was. But to a large extent, the *management* of the U.S.'s largest companies has been the critical determinant of their success or failure.

Consider the locomotive business. American Locomotive and Baldwin Locomotive got creamed; their managements stuck too long with the steam engine. But General Motors' management foresaw the promise of the diesel, and GM's Electro-Motive division prospered. Two other railroad equipment manufacturers, Pullman and American Car & Foundry (now ACF Industries), diversified successfully.

In growth industries, too, there are winners and losers. Take aircraft: Curtiss-Wright was by far the largest aircraft company at the end of World War II, but its president, Roy T. Hurley, failed to get his company into jet manufacturing until 1952—too late. He apparently figured that an improved piston engine would compete successfully with the jet, and Curtiss-Wright slipped from twenty-eighth among U.S. industrial corporations in 1945 right off the top one hundred. Boeing Company, by contrast, wasn't even on the list of one hundred in 1945, was forty-first in 1967, is ninety-fourth today.

In the supercharged data processing business, International Business Machines moved up from ninety-fourth in 1945 to fifth today; Burroughs and Honeywell have both vaulted into the ranks of the top one hundred; Xerox came from nowhere to thirtieth place. Not every big company fared so well in data processing, however. Singer's Donald Kircher led his company into minicomputers and point-of-sale terminals—with disastrous results. Once sixteenth among U.S. corporations, Singer is no longer on the list of the top one hundred.

The top ranks of U.S. industry are clearly shifting more than the system's critics imagine. This is not to say that giant companies go out of business as quickly and easily as small businesses do; yet, on this record, they are very far from being invulnerable to changing technology and changing consumer tastes and to poor management.

TABLE A-1 THE TOP 100 INDUSTRIALS—1917

	Company	Assets[a] (millions)	Revenues[b] (millions)	Net Income[c] (millions)
1.	U.S. Steel	$2,450	$1,285	$224.2
2.	Standard Oil (N.J.) (now Exxon Corp.)[d]	574	412	80.8
3.	Bethlehem Steel	382	299	27.3
4.	Armour & Company	314	577	21.3
5.	Swift & Company (now Esmark)	306	875	34.6
6.	International Harvester	265	166	14.0
7.	E. I. du Pont de Nemours[e]	263	270	45.6
8.	Midvale Steel & Ordnance	256	NA	35.6
9.	U.S. Rubber (now Uniroyal)	250	176	15.3
10.	General Electric	232	197	26.9
11.	Int'l Mercantile Marine	231	42	11.8
12.	American Smelting & Rfg. (now ASARCO)	222	441	18.5
13.	Anaconda Copper Mining	216	156	34.3
14.	Standard Oil (N.Y.)	204	NA	21.8
15.	Phelps Dodge	187	60	22.5
16.	Singer Manufacturing (now Singer Company)[f]	182	113	d0.7
17.	Jones & Laughlin Steel[f]	168	130	26.6

18.	Westinghouse Elec. & Mfg. (now Westinghouse Electric Corp.)	165	96	15.4
19.	American Tobacco (now American Brands)	164	90	13.3
20.	Ford Motor[g]	160	275	30.3
21.	Union Carbide & Carbon (now Union Carbide Corp.)	157	NA	9.6
22.	Cambria Steel (controlled by Midvale Steel)	147	NA	25.7
23.	B. F. Goodrich	146	87	10.4
24.	Central Leather	145	92	14.4
25.	Kennecott Copper	143	23	18.0
26.	Pullman	141	49	13.6
27.	Consolidation Coal	138	26	8.5
28.	American Sugar Refining (now Amstar)	137	200E	8.2
29.	Chile Copper	136	19	2.6
30.	General Motors	134	173	27.7
31.	American Can	133	134E	11.9

Figures are as of 12/31/1917, except when fiscal year was used.
NA = not available; E = estimated; d = deficit.
[a] Excludes reserves for depreciation and depletion where possible.
[b] Excludes excise taxes.
[c] After depreciation, fixed charges, and taxes, but before preferred and common dividends.
[d] Revenues include proportionate share of earnings of affiliate companies.
[e] Assets include depreciation charges not categorized.
[f] Consolidated to include foreign subsidiaries.
[g] Figures unconsolidated; parent company only.

TABLE A-1 THE TOP 100 INDUSTRIALS—1917—(Continued)

	Company	Assets[a] (millions)	Revenues[b] (millions)	Net Income[c] (millions)
32.	Sears, Roebuck	130	178	14.1
33.	Texas Company (now Texaco)	129	54	19.7
34.	American Car & Foundry (now ACF Industries)	127	108	11.3
35.	Standard Oil (Calif.)	127	79	19.0
36.	Standard Oil (Ind.)	127	190	25.4
37.	Magnolia Petroleum	123	NA	10.2
38.	American Woolen	122	150E	6.8
39.	Pittsburgh Coal	113	50	14.1
40.	Willys-Overland	113	NA	6.1
41.	Corn Products Refining (now CPC International)	112	100E	11.3
42.	Ohio Cities Gas	112	40	10.3
43.	Republic Iron & Steel (now Republic Steel)	112	78	15.9
44.	United Fruit (now United Brands)	110	NA	13.0
45.	Liggett & Myers Tobacco (now Liggett Group)	108	66	7.4
46.	Virginia Carolina Chem.	107	90E	8.4
47.	Aluminum Co. of America	104	NA	16.4
48.	Lackawanna Steel	104	77	16.1

		Assets	Revenues	Net Income
49.	Gulf Oil	103	71	16.7
50.	Prairie Oil & Gas	103	NA	NA
51.	Wilson & Co.	102	175E	6.5
52.	W. R. Grace	97	200E	12.0E
53.	Youngstown Sheet & Tube	97	98	38.4
54.	Western Electric (controlled by American Telephone & Telegraph)	96	152	2.9
55.	Colorado Fuel & Iron (now CF&I Steel)	95	40	4.0
56.	Great Northern Iron Ore[h]	94	9	4.5
57.	Procter & Gamble	88	129	7.1
58.	Atl., Gulf & W. Indies SS	87	48	9.6
59.	Crucible Steel	87	NA	12.3
60.	Ohio Oil (now Marathon Oil)	85	27	13.6
61.	American Locomotive	84	82	7.2
62.	F. W. Woolworth	84	98	9.3
63.	Cuba Cane Sugar	83	NA	7.3
64.	Mexican Petroleum (controlled by Pan American Petroleum & Transport Co.)	83	18	5.0
65.	Morris & Company	83	234E	5.4

[h] Trust created and certificates distributed to stockholders of Great Northern Railway Company. Assets are those reported to the trustees and their interest in the properties. Revenues are the total receipts of the properties. Net income is the earnings of the properties accruing to the trust.

TABLE A-1 THE TOP 100 INDUSTRIALS—1917—(Continued)

	Company	Assets[a] (millions)	Revenues[b] (millions)	Net Income[c] (millions)
66.	Amer. Agricultural Chem.	82	NA	5.5
67.	Lehigh Coal & Navigation	81	22	3.4
68.	National Lead (now NL Industries)	81	74	4.9
69.	Sinclair Oil & Refining	81	45	9.1
70.	Utah Copper	81	49	30.0
71.	International Paper	80	NA	8.9
72.	U.S. Smelt., Rfg. & Min. (now UV Industries)	80	35	3.5
73.	Goodyear Tire & Rubber	79	111	14.0
74.	Union Oil of California	78	34	7.6
75.	Vacuum Oil	76	NA	9.3
76.	National Biscuit (now Nabisco)	74	58	4.6
77.	United Shoe Machinery	74	22	5.4
78.	Baldwin Locomotive	73	98	8.3
79.	Deere & Company	70	32	4.9
80.	Studebaker	70	50	3.5
81.	International Nickel (now Inco Ltd.)	67	34	10.1

82.	R. J. Reynolds Tobacco (now R. J. Reynolds Industries)	66	71	8.6
83.	Associated Oil	65	28	3.8
84.	Cudahy Packing	65	185	1.4
85.	Eastman Kodak	64	NA	14.5
86.	P. Lorillard	63	NA	5.9
87.	Atlantic Refining (now Atlantic Richfield)	61	86	9.0
88.	Calumet & Hecla Mining	60E	17	12.2
89.	Greene Cananea Copper	59	9	2.5
90.	General Chemical	57	NA	7.7
91.	Inland Steel	57	NA	10.5
92.	United Motors	56	35	7.3
93.	Allis-Chalmers	55	26	4.0
94.	American Cotton Oil	55	NA	1.5
95.	Crane	54	NA	NA
96.	Libby, McNeill & Libby (controlled by Swift & Co.)	54	300E	NA
97.	Sinclair Gulf	54	11	1.1
98.	Distillers Securities (now National Distillers & Chemical)	53	NA	4.8
99.	Pan Amer. Pet. & Trans.	52	7	4.3
100.	Utd. Verde Extension Mining	52	15	-8.3

TABLE A-1 THE TOP 100 INDUSTRIALS—1917—(Continued)

Company	Assets[a] (millions)	Revenues[b] (millions)	Net Income[c] (millions)
The Runners-Up of 1917			
101. Firestone Tire & Rubber			
102. Maxwell Motor			
103. Cosden & Co.			
104. Tide Water Oil			
105. Prairie Pipe Line			
106. Calumet & Ariz. Mng.			
107. Lake Superior Company			
108. Pierce Oil			
109. Borden			
110. National Aniline			

TABLE A-2 THE TOP 100 INDUSTRIALS—1929

Company	Assets[a] (millions)	Revenues[b] (millions)	Net Income[c] (millions)
1. U.S. Steel	$2,286	$1,097	$197.5
2. Standard Oil (N.J.) (now Exxon Corp.)	1,767	1,523	120.9
3. General Motors	1,131	1,504	247.3
4. Standard Oil (Ind.)	874	495	83.0
5. Bethlehem Steel	802	343	42.2
6. Ford Motor[a]	761	1,143	88.4
7. Standard Oil (N.Y.)	708	NA	38.8
8. Anaconda Copper Mining	681	306	69.1
9. Texas Corp. (now Texaco)	610	213	48.3
10. Standard Oil (Calif.)	605	190	46.6
11. General Electric	516	415	67.3
12. E. I. du Pont de Nemours	497	200E	72.3

Figures are as of 12/31/1929, except when fiscal year was used.
NA = not available; E = estimated; d = deficit.
[a] Excludes reserves for depreciation and depletion where possible.
[b] Excludes excise taxes.
[c] After depreciation, fixed charges, and taxes, but before preferred and common dividends.
[a] Figures unconsolidated; parent company only.

TABLE A-2 THE TOP 100 INDUSTRIALS—1929—(Continued)

	Company	Assets[a] (millions)	Revenues[b] (millions)	Net Income[c] (millions)
13.	Shell Union Oil (now Shell Oil)	486	245	17.6
14.	Armour & Co.	452	1,000	9.8
15.	Gulf Oil	431	272	44.5
16.	Sinclair Consol. Oil	401	197	16.6
17.	Int'l Harvester	384	337	36.8
18.	Swift & Co. (now Esmark)	351	1,000E	13.1
19.	Kennecott Copper	338	116	52.1
20.	Republic Steel	332	NA	20.5
21.	Pullman	316	NA	17.7
22.	Western Electric (controlled by American Telephone & Telegraph)	309	411	27.0
23.	U.S. Rubber (now Uniroyal)	308	193	0.6
24.	Union Carbide & Carbon (now Union Carbide Corp.)	307	142	33.6
25.	International Paper[e]	283	NA	2.7
26.	Allied Chemical & Dye (now Allied Chemical Corp.)	277	NA	30.2
27.	Singer Manufacturing (now Singer Co.)[f]	269	132	27.5
28.	American Tobacco (now American Brands)	265	NA	30.2

29.	Westinghouse Elec. & Mfg. (now Westinghouse Electric Corp.)	254	216	27.1
30.	Sears, Roebuck	252	444	30.1
31.	Tide Water Associated Oil	251	176	14.0
32.	Koppers	250E	NA	NA
33.	Goodyear Tire & Rubber	243	256	18.6
34.	American Smelting & Rfg. (now ASARCO)	241	NA	21.8
35.	Union Oil of California	241	89	15.0
36.	Humble Oil & Refining [controlled by Standard Oil (N.J.)]	240	199	32.3
37.	Paramount Pictures	237	152	15.5
38.	Youngstown Sheet & Tube	236	161	21.6
39.	Aluminum Co. of America	235	107	25.3
40.	United Fruit (now United Brands)	226	NA	17.8
41.	Jones & Laughlin Steel	222	135	20.8
42.	International Match	218	NA	20.6
43.	Pure Oil	215	77	6.5
44.	Chrysler	210	375	21.9
45.	Prairie Oil & Gas	210	132	13.9
46.	Vacuum Oil	206	NA	36.8

e 99% owned by International Paper & Power Co. in 1929. Figures are for International Paper Co. only.
f Consolidated to include foreign subsidiaries.

TABLE A-2   THE TOP 100 INDUSTRIALS—1929—(Continued)

	Company	Assets[a] (millions)	Revenues[b] (millions)	Net Income[c] (millions)
47.	Amer. Rad. & Std. Sanit. (now American Standard)	199	182	20.0
48.	Continental Oil	197	82	9.0
49.	American Can	191	157E	22.7
50.	Montgomery Ward	188	292	13.4
51.	International Nickel (now Inco Ltd.)	182	66	22.2
52.	National Dairy Products (now Kraft)	180	300	21.6
53.	Borden	175	329	20.4
54.	Pittsburgh Coal	172	46	d
55.	Atlantic Refining (now Atlantic Richfield)	167	154	17.3
56.	Warner Brothers Pictures	167	72	17.3
57.	Glen Alden Coal (for 1930)	166	73	12.2
58.	F. W. Woolworth	165	303	35.7
59.	B. F. Goodrich	164	165	7.4
60.	Eastman Kodak	163	NA	22.0
61.	R. J. Reynolds Tobacco (now R. J. Reynolds Industries)	163	266	32.2
62.	Firestone Tire & Rubber	162	145	7.7

63.	United Cigar Stores of America	162	NA	NA
64.	Radio Corp. of America (now RCA Corp.)	159	182	15.9
65.	American Sugar Refining (now Amstar)	157	143	6.6
66.	Liggett & Myers Tobacco (now Liggett Group)	150	120	22.0
67.	Great Atl. & Pac. Tea	147	1,054	26.2
68.	Phillips Petroleum	145	52	13.2
69.	Prairie Pipe Line	141	40	22.8
70.	Marshall Field	137	180	9.2
71.	Studebaker	134	145	11.3
72.	National Biscuit (now Nabisco)	133	139	21.4
73.	Richfield Oil	132	83	8.6
74.	Phila. & Reading Coal & Iron	129	65	d0.8
75.	Wheeling Steel (now Wheeling-Pittsburgh Steel)	128	85	8.0
76.	Corn Products Refining (now CPC International)	127	80	16.3
77.	Phelps Dodge	125	40	5.4
78.	Crucible Steel	124	NA	8.2
79.	Loew's (now Metro-Goldwyn-Mayer)	124	116	10.9
80.	National Steel	121	NA	11.8
81.	American Car & Foundry (now ACF Industries)	119	80	5.4
82.	Crown Zellerbach	119	NA	4.4
83.	United Drug (now Dart Industries)	118	106	6.1
84.	Crane	116	NA	11.6

TABLE A-2 THE TOP 100 INDUSTRIALS—1929—(Continued)

	Company	Assets[a] (millions)	Revenues[b] (millions)	Net Income[c] (millions)
85.	Long Bell Lumber	116	28	1.7
86.	American Woolen	114	207E	d4.2
87.	Sinclair Crude Oil Purch.[g]	112	71	d0.6
88.	International Shoe (now Interco)	111	132	17.0
89.	Ohio Oil (now Marathon Oil)	111	83	12.3
90.	S. S. Kresge (now K Mart)	110	156	15.0
91.	Gen'l Theatres Equip.	109	11	4.9
92.	Procter & Gamble	109	202	19.1
93.	National Lead (now NL Industries)	108	111	10.2
94.	P. Lorillard	107	NA	1.3
95.	American Locomotive	106	57	6.9
96.	American Rolling Mill (now Armco Steel)	104	70	6.1
97.	Inland Steel	103	69	11.7
98.	Pittsburgh Plate Glass (now PPG Industries)	102	171	11.7
99.	Cuba Cane Sugar	101	26	d0.8
100.	Baldwin Locomotive	99	43	2.3

The Runners-Up of 1929

101. Cleveland-Cliffs Iron
102. Utah Copper
103. Wilson & Co.
104. Hudson Coal
105. Deere & Co.
106. Nevada Copper
107. Consolidation Co.
108. United Shoe Machinery
109. Sun Oil
110. Mexican Petroleum

[a] Jointly owned by Standard Oil (Ind.) and Sinclair Consolidated Oil in 1929.

TABLE A-3 THE TOP 100 INDUSTRIALS—1945

	Company	Assets[a] (millions)	Revenues[b] (millions)	Net Income[c] (millions)
1.	Standard Oil (N.J.) (now Exxon Corp.)	$2,532	$1,618	$154.2
2.	U.S. Steel	1,891	1,747	58.0
3.	General Motors	1,808	3,128	i74.4
4.	Socony-Vacuum Oil (now Mobil Corp.)	1,044	829	41.5
5.	E. I. du Pont de Nemours	1,025	611	77.5
6.	Standard Oil (Ind.)	946	620	50.3
7.	Bethlehem Steel	881	1,327	34.9
8.	General Electric	858	1,466	58.3
9.	Texas Co. (now Texaco)	854	556	51.9
10.	Ford Motor[d]	816	897	8.6
11.	Standard Oil (Calif.)	738	343	55.6
12.	Gulf Oil	653	505	45.2
13.	Anaconda Copper Mining	616	328	20.4
14.	International Harvester	591	622	24.5
15.	Humble Oil & Refining [controlled by Standard Oil (N.J.)]	560	443	70.9
16.	Sears, Roebuck	528	1,045	35.8

17.	American Tobacco (now American Brands)	484	275	19.7
18.	Kennecott Copper	465	210	30.3
19.	Western Electric (controlled by American Telephone & Telegraph)	464	861	15.1
20.	Sinclair Oil	456	406	29.3
21.	Westinghouse Electric	450	685	19.8
22.	Shell Union Oil (now Shell Oil)	435	476	28.8
23.	Union Carbide & Carbon (now Union Carbide Corp.)	428	482	37.9
24.	Aluminum Co. of America	427	89	20.0
25.	Chrysler	414	995	32.5
26.	Republic Steel	413	498	22.9
27.	Montgomery Ward	369	655	9.5
28.	Curtiss-Wright	354	1,198	24.4
29.	Swift & Co. (now Esmark)	353	1,308	12.3
30.	Armour & Co.	349	1,213	9.2
31.	Goodyear Tire & Rubber	341	716	15.1

Figures are as of 12/31/1945, except when fiscal year was used.
NA = not available.
[a] Excludes reserves for depreciation and depletion where possible; U.S. Treasury Tax notes, if deducted from liabilities, were added back to assets.
[b] Excludes excise taxes.
[c] After depreciation, fixed charges, and taxes, but before preferred and common dividends.
[d] Figures unconsolidated, parent company only. Net income after tax credit of $23.6 million; company had net loss of $15 million before taxes.

TABLE A-3 THE TOP 100 INDUSTRIALS—1945—(Continued)

	Company	Assets[a] (millions)	Revenues[b] (millions)	Net Income[c] (millions)
32.	Phillips Petroleum	317	213	22.6
33.	R. J. Reynolds Tobacco (now R. J. Reynolds Industries)	315	221	19.7
34.	Eastman Kodak	307	302	25.7
35.	Firestone Tire & Rubber	300	682	16.4
36.	F. W. Woolworth	297	477	23.6
37.	International Nickel (now Inco Ltd.)	294	148	25.0
38.	Liggett & Myers Tobacco (now Liggett Group)	293	193	14.9
39.	Allied Chemical & Dye (now Allied Chemical Corp.)	286	268	18.9
40.	Jones & Laughlin Steel	276	285	8.1
41.	Pullman	273	148	13.9
42.	Atlantic Refining (now Atlantic Richfield)	272	259	8.5
43.	National Steel	261	272	11.1
44.	Bendix Aviation (now Bendix Corp.)	260	649	13.3
45.	International Paper	259	234	8.5
46.	U.S. Rubber (now Uniroyal)	243	478	13.0
47.	National Dairy Products (now Kraft)	242	633	14.1

48.	Youngstown Sheet & Tube	240	230	7.5
49.	United Fruit (now United Brands)	235	NA	18.9
50.	Tide Water Associated Oil	233	244	18.1
51.	American Can	232	242	13.3
52.	Great Atl. & Pac. Tea	231	1,435	12.3
53.	Union Oil of California	229	135	9.2
54.	Singer Manufacturing (now Singer Co.)^e	225	221	14.3
55.	B. F. Goodrich	223	372	12.3
56.	Pure Oil	215	165	13.6
57.	American Rolling Mill (now Armco Steel)	207	220	13.4
58.	Loew's (now Metro-Goldwyn-Mayer)	207	154	12.9
59.	Amer. Smelting & Rfg. (now ASARCO)	201	144	11.5
60.	Allis-Chalmers	198	290	7.1
61.	Sun Oil (now Sun Co.)	197	472	15.7
62.	Warner Brother Pictures	196	147	9.9
63.	Deere & Co.	195	138	8.7
64.	Phelps Dodge	195	138	10.1
65.	J. C. Penney	194	549	17.4
66.	Distillers Corp.-Seagrams (now Seagram Co.)	191	158	13.8
67.	Inland Steel	191	217	9.9

^{e} Consolidated to include foreign subsidiaries.

TABLE A-3 THE TOP 100 INDUSTRIALS—1945—(*Continued*)

	Company	Assets[a] (millions)	Revenues[b] (millions)	Net Income[c] (millions)
68.	Procter & Gamble	188	343	19.5
69.	Schenley Distillers	187	215	23.9
70.	Borden	180	459	12.1
71.	United Aircraft (now United Technologies)	179	484	12.9
72.	Continental Can (now Continental Group)	178	206	5.8
73.	Continental Oil	173	144	15.1
74.	Coca-Cola	169	149	25.1
75.	S. S. Kresge (now K Mart)	168	223	10.7
76.	Paramount Pictures	168	158	15.4
77.	General Foods	163	307	13.1
78.	Lockheed Aircraft	163	418	5.5
79.	Weyerhaeuser Timber (now Weyerhaeuser Co.)	162	61	8.1
80.	Radio Corp. of America (now RCA Corp.)	160	278	11.3
81.	Anderson, Clayton	157	246	6.0
82.	Douglas Aircraft	156	745	9.0
83.	Pittsburgh Plate Glass (now PPG Industries)	154	144	13.5
84.	American Car & Foundry (now ACF Industries)	150	118	5.3

85.	Twentieth Century-Fox	149	178	12.7
86.	Celanese	147	104	7.6
87.	American Cyanamid	145	159	6.2
88.	Hearst Consol. Publ. (wholly owned by Hearst Corp.)	143	109	7.5
89.	Standard Oil (Ohio)	142	146	3.7
90.	American Viscose (now A.V.C. Corp.)	140	119	10.2
91.	Glenn L. Martin	138	356	9.4
92.	Wheeling Steel (now Wheeling-Pittsburgh Steel)	136	143	4.0
93.	National Distillers Products (now National Distillers & Chemical)	135	180	11.8
94.	IBM	134	142	10.9
95.	National Biscuit (now Nabisco)	132	205	10.5
96.	Ohio Oil (now Marathon Oil)	132	83	13.9
97.	Philip Morris	131	84	6.1
98.	United Shoe Machinery	131	59	7.5
99.	Dow Chemical	129	102	7.0
100.	National Lead (now NL Industries)	129	168	6.5

The Runners-Up of 1945

101.	Wilson & Co.
102.	American Locomotive

TABLE A-3 THE TOP 100 INDUSTRIALS—1945—*(Continued)*

Company	Assets[a] (millions)	Revenues[b] (millions)	Net Income[c] (millions)
103. American Radiator			
104. American Sugar			
105. Consolidated Vultee			
106. Crane			
107. Owens-Illinois Glass			
108. Safeway Stores			
109. Corn Products Rfg.			
110. May Department Stores			

TABLE A-4 THE TOP 100 INDUSTRIALS—1966

	Company	Assets[a] (millions)	Revenues[b] (millions)	Net Income[c] (millions)
1.	Standard Oil (N.J.) (now Exxon Corp.)	$13,853	$12,191	$1,090.9
2.	General Motors	12,916	20,209	1,793.4
2.	Ford Motor	8,090	12,240	621.0
4.	Texaco	6,363	4,427	692.1
5.	Gulf Oil	5,892	3,782	504.8
6.	U.S. Steel	5,750	4,355	249.2
7.	Sears, Roebuck	5,285	6,805	321.5
8.	Mobil Oil (now Mobil Corp.)	5,512	5,254	356.1
9.	General Electric	4,852	7,177	338.9
10.	IBM	4,661	4,248	526.1
11.	General Tele. & Elec.[d]	4,511	2,391	198.7

Figures are as of 12/31/1966, except when fiscal year was used.

d = deficit.

[a] Excludes reserves for depreciation and depletion where possible; includes U.S. Treasury notes, if deducted from liabilities and added back to assets.

[b] Excludes excise taxes.

[c] After depreciation, fixed charges and taxes, but before preferred and common dividends.

[d] Considered a public utility in prior periods.

TABLE A-4 THE TOP 100 INDUSTRIALS—1966—(Continued)

	Company	Assets[a] (millions)	Revenues[b] (millions)	Net Income[c] (millions)
12.	Standard Oil (Calif.)	4,502	2,698	424.0
13.	Standard Oil (Ind.)	3,849	2,709	255.9
14.	Chrysler	3,149	5,650	189.2
15.	Shell Oil	3,035	2,790	255.2
16.	E. I. du Pont de Nemours	3,016	3,185	389.1
17.	Tenneco[a]	2,909	1,164	108.1
18.	Phillips Petroleum	2,673	1,686	144.5
19.	Bethlehem Steel	2,555	2,669	170.9
20.	Western Electric (wholly owned by American Telephone & Telegraph)	2,498	3,624	173.1
21.	Union Carbide	2,418	2,224	231.0
22.	Int'l Tel. & Tel.[a]	2,360	2,121	89.9
23.	Continental Oil	2,070	1,749	115.6
24.	Aluminum Co. of America	1,940	1,373	106.1
25.	Westinghouse Electric	1,932	2,581	119.7
26.	Goodyear Tire & Rubber	1,912	2,476	118.5
27.	Union Oil of Calif.	1,899	1,364	134.2

TABLE A-4 THE TOP 100 INDUSTRIALS—19__

	Company	Assets[a] (millions)	Revenues[b] (millions)	Income (millions)
49.	R. J. Reynolds Tobacco (now R. J. Reynolds Industries)	1,205	1,094	137.9
50.	Deere & Co.	1,173	1,062	78.7
51.	Olin Mathieson Chem. (now Olin Corp.)	1,163	1,117	66.7
52.	Kaiser Alum. & Chem.	1,134	782	58.9
53.	National Steel	1,129	1,051	71.9
54.	Caterpillar Tractor	1,118	1,524	150.1
55.	Jones & Laughlin Steel	1,110	1,010	65.1
56.	American Can	1,087	1,370	71.6
57.	Kennecott Copper	1,075	740	125.4
58.	United Aircraft (now United Technologies)	1,046	1,663	46.5
59.	American Tobacco (now American Brands)	1,033	919	86.0
60.	Sperry Rand	1,033	1,487	53.9
61.	International Nickel (now Inco Ltd.)	1,023	694	118.2
62.	Inland Steel	1,019	1,054	68.1
63.	Uniroyal	1,011	1,321	45.3
64.	Tidewater Oil	1,011	696	71.9

65.	Weyerhaeuser	997	838	79.2
66.	Burlington Industries	992	1,372	77.1
67.	Singer	983	1,049	47.3
68.	F. W. Woolworth	976	1,573	67.7
69.	Continental Can (now Continental Group)	957	1,339	70.9
70.	Georgia-Pacific	953	659	50.3
71.	Minnesota Mining & Mfg.	953	1,153	138.5
72.	Youngstown Sheet & Tube	953	762	42.8
73.	Pittsburgh Plate Glass (now PPG Industries)	950	942	49.5
74.	General Foods	929	1,652	98.8
75.	American Cyanamid	911	953	94.4
76.	Borden	910	1,546	57.7
77.	National Dairy Products (now Kraft)	885	2,252	73.5
78.	Distillers Corp.-Seagrams (now Seagram Co.)	883	467	45.1
79.	Crown Zellerbach	874	764	53.7
80.	Marathon Oil	872	622	68.8
81.	Great Atl. & Pac. Tea	863	5,475	56.2
82.	Owens-Illinois	863	908	54.2
83.	B. F. Goodrich	850	1,039	48.6
84.	Douglas Aircraft	850	1,048	d27.6
85.	J. C. Penney	817	2,549	79.1
86.	U.S. Plywood (now Champion International)	798	1,029	43.3

TABLE A-4   THE TOP 100 INDUSTRIALS—1966—(Continued)

	Company	Assets[a] (millions)	Revenues[b] (millions)	Net Income[c] (millions)
87.	Federated Dept. Stores	775	1,412	73.6
88.	Honeywell	772	914	45.3
89.	May Dept. Stores	759	979	38.4
90.	National Distillers & Chem.	743	547	40.7
91.	Litton Industries	743	1,172	55.6
92.	General Dynamics	734	1,797	58.4
93.	Lockheed Aircraft	727	2,085	58.9
94.	St. Regis Paper	726	700	38.7
95.	Swift & Co. (now Esmark)	718	2,970	19.8
96.	Allied Stores	710	1,030	22.7
97.	Corn Products (now CPC International)	703	1,048	58.2
98.	FMC	694	1,010	62.9
99.	Armour & Co.	686	2,280	24.7
100.	Sunray DX Oil	686	525	44.8

101. General Tire & Rubber
102. Signal Oil & Gas
103. Borg Warner
104. Allis-Chalmers
105. Coca-Cola
106. Bendix
107. Xerox
108. Kimberly-Clark
109. Safeway Stores
110. Standard Oil (Ohio)
111. American Metal Climax
112. Chas. Pfizer
113. General American Transportation
114. Phelps Dodge
115. North American Aviation
116. United Merch. & Manufacturers
117. National Cash Register
118. American Home Products
119. Scott Paper
120. American Smelting & Rfg.

TABLE A-4 THE TOP 100 INDUSTRIALS—1966—(Continued)

Company	Assets[a] (millions)	Revenues[b] (millions)	Net Income[c] (millions)
121. Skelly Oil			
122. Schenley Industries			
123. Kaiser Industries			
124. J. P. Stevens			
125. Kaiser Steel			

TABLE A-5 THE TOP 100 INDUSTRIALS—1977

	Company	Assets[a] (millions)	Revenues[b] (millions)	Net Income[c] (millions)
1.	Exxon	$36,331	$48,631	$2,641.0
2.	General Motors	24,343	47,181	2,902.8
3.	Mobil Corp.	18,767	26,063	942.5
4.	Texaco	18,194	26,452	869.7
5.	IBM	17,723	16,304	2,398.1
6.	Ford Motor	15,749	28,840	983.1
7.	Standard Oil (Calif.)	13,765	19,434	880.1
8.	General Telephone & Elec.	13,601	6,751	453.2
9.	Gulf Oil	13,449	16,451	816.0
10.	Sears, Roebuck	12,711	14,950	694.5
11.	General Electric	12,050	15,697	930.6
12.	Standard Oil (Ind.)	11,213	11,532	893.0
13.	Int'l. Tel. & Tel.	11,070	11,764	494.5

Figures are as of 12/31/76, except when fiscal year was used.
[a] Total assets as reported by company.
[b] Excludes excise taxes.
[c] After depreciation, fixed charges, and taxes, but before preferred and common dividends.

TABLE A-5 THE TOP 100 INDUSTRIALS—1977—(Continued)

Company	Assets[a] (millions)	Revenues[b] (millions)	Net Income[c] (millions)
14. U.S. Steel	9,168	8,604	410.3
15. Atlantic Richfield	8,853	8,463	575.2
16. Shell Oil	7,837	9,230	705.8
17. Tenneco	7,177	6,389	383.5
18. Chrysler	7,074	15,538	328.2
19. E. I. du Pont de Nemours	7,018	8,361	459.3
20. Dow Chemical	6,849	5,652	612.8
21. Union Carbide	6,622	6,346	441.2
22. Standard Oil (Ohio)	6,260	2,916	136.9
23. Continental Oil	6,042	7,958	460.0
24. Eastman Kodak	5,517	5,438	650.6
25. Westinghouse Electric	5,318	6,145	223.2
26. Western Electric (wholly owned by American Telephone & Telegraph)	5,178	6,931	203.6
27. Phillips Petroleum	5,068	5,698	411.7
28. Bethlehem Steel	4,939	5,248	168.0
29. Sun Company	4,836	5,387	356.2

30.	Xerox	4,612	4,404	358.9
31.	Goodyear Tire & Rubber	4,336	5,791	122.0
32.	R. J. Reynolds Industries	4,277	4,291	353.9
33.	Union Oil of Calif.	4,227	5,351	268.8
34.	Procter & Gamble	4,103	6,513	401.1
35.	Monsanto	3,958	4,270	366.3
36.	Occidental Petroleum	3,905	5,534	183.7
37.	Caterpillar Tractor	3,894	5,042	383.2
38.	RCA	3,836	5,329	177.4
39.	Weyerhaeuser	3,682	2,868	306.0
40.	International Paper	3,640	3,541	253.6
41.	Getty Oil	3,629	3,059	258.5
42.	Inco Ltd.	3,628	2,040	196.8
43.	Cities Service	3,615	3,965	217.0
44.	Philip Morris	3,582	3,134	265.7
45.	International Harvester	3,575	5,488	174.1
46.	Aluminum Co. of America	3,570	2,924	143.8
47.	J. C. Penny	3,484	8,354	228.1
48.	Gulf & Western Inds.	3,480	3,396	200.2
49.	Minnesota Mining & Mfg.	3,324	3,514	338.5
50.	Firestone Tire & Rubber	3,261	3,939	96.0
51.	Marathon Oil	3,043	3,488	195.8

TABLE A-5 THE TOP 100 INDUSTRIALS—1977—(Continued)

	Company	Assets[a] (millions)	Revenues[b] (millions)	Net Income[c] (millions)
52.	Deere & Co.	2,893	3,134	241.6
53.	Rockwell Int'l.	2,889	5,195	123.4
54.	K Mart	2,866	8,484	266.6
55.	Sperry Rand	2,841	3,270	156.8
56.	Armco Steel	2,834	3,151	119.8
57.	AMAX	2,799	1,170	150.1
58.	National Steel	2,798	2,841	85.7
59.	Amerada Hess	2,777	3,915	152.6
60.	W. R. Grace	2,756	3,615	131.9
61.	United Technologies	2,626	5,166	157.4
62.	Georgia-Pacific	2,584	3,038	215.3
63.	Halliburton	2,553	4,866	305.5
64.	Burroughs	2,539	1,871	185.9
65.	American Brands	2,456	2,672	122.0
66.	Allied Chemical	2,439	2,630	126.3
67.	IC Industries[d]	2,353	1,689	60.8
68.	General Foods	2,345	4,910	177.3

69.	Reynolds Metals	2,342	2,084	75.1
70.	Republic Steel	2,333	2,546	65.9
71.	NCR	2,312	2,313	90.0
72.	Kennecott Copper	2,308	956	8.8
73.	Federated Dept. Stores	2,269	4,447	168.1
74.	Honeywell	2,204	2,495	105.3
75.	Owens-Illinois	2,195	2,590	106.7
76.	Continental Group	2,189	3,458	118.3
77.	Kaiser Alum. & Chemical	2,181	1,852	44.5
78.	Champion International	2,180	2,911	103.1
79.	Pfizer	2,173	1,888	159.9
80.	Seagram	2,161	1,092	80.5
81.	LTV	2,135	4,497	30.7
82.	McDonnell Douglas	2,130	3,544	108.9
83.	Beatrice Foods	2,129	5,289	182.6
84.	Ashland Oil	2,105	4,087	136.0
85.	F. W. Woolworth	2,093	5,152	108.2
86.	Inland Steel	2,069	2,388	104.0
87.	Litton Industries	2,057	3,355	11.8
88.	PPG Industries	2,033	2,255	151.5
89.	American Cyanamid	2,002	2,094	135.8

[a] Considered a railroad in prior periods.

TABLE A-5 THE TOP 100 INDUSTRIALS—1977—(Continued)

	Company	Assets[a] (millions)	Revenues[b] (millions)	Net Income[c] (millions)
90.	Schlumberger	1,995	1,810	293.2
91.	American Can	1,956	3,143	100.9
92.	Warner-Lambert	1,930	2,349	159.7
93.	FMC	1,920	2,145	80.2
94.	Boeing	1,919	3,919	102.9
95.	Celanese	1,910	2,123	69.0
96.	Coca-Cola	1,903	3,033	285.0
97.	TRW	1,870	2,929	133.1
98.	Signal Companies	1,869	2,480	64.8
99.	Engelhard Min. & Chem.	1,853	6,464	124.9
100.	Kraft	1,822	4,977	135.7

The Runners-Up of 1977

101. Pennzoil
102. Borden
103. Merck

104. Colgate-Palmolive
105. Lykes Corp.
106. Phelps Dodge
107. Esmark
108. Ingersoll-Rand
109. Burlington Industries
110. Boise Cascade
111. Johnson & Johnson
112. Dresser Industries
113. Safeway Stores
114. Williams Companies
115. Bendix
116. Uniroyal
117. Crown Zellerbach
118. Kerr-McGee
119. Singer
120. Lockheed Aircraft
121. Eli Lilly
122. B. F. Goodrich
123. Ralston Purina
124. ASARCO
125. General Tire & Rubber

TABLE A-6 THE TOP 100 SURVIVORS, DROPOUTS, AND NEWCOMERS

Each of the 209 companies listed alphabetically below has appeared on one or more of the listings of the top 100 industrial companies in the United States. After each name appears the ranking it attained in each period in accordance with its asset size.

Company	1917	1929	1945	1966	1977
Allied Chemical & Dye (allied Chemical)	—	26	39	37	66
Allied Stores	—	—	—	96	—
Allis Chalmers	93	—	60	—	—
Aluminum Co. of America	47	39	24	24	46
AMAX	—	—	—	—	57
Amerada Hess	—	—	—	—	59
American Agricultural Chem.[1]	66	—	—	—	—
American Can	31	49	51	56	91
American Car & Foundry[2]	34	81	84	—	—
American Cotton Oil[3]	94	—	—	—	—
American Cyanamid	—	—	87	75	89
American Locomotive[4]	61	95	—	—	—
American Radiator & Std. Sanitary[5]	—	47	—	—	—
American Rolling Mill (Armco Steel)	—	96	57	48	56
American Smelting & Rfg.[6]	12	34	59	—	—

American Sugar Refining[7]	28	65	—	—	—
American Tobacco (Amer. Brands)	19	28	17	59	65
American Viscose[8]	—	86	90	—	—
American Woolen[9]	38	8	13	45	—
Anaconda Copper Mining (Anaconda Co.)[10]	13	—	81	—	—
Anderson, Clayton	—	14	30	99	—
Armour & Co.[11]	4	—	—	—	84
Ashland Oil	—	—	—	—	—
Associated Oil[12]	83	—	—	—	—
Atl. Gulf & West Indies S.S. Lines[13]	58	—	—	—	—
Atlantic Refining (Atlantic Richfield)	87	55	42	36	15

[1] American Agricultural Chemical transferred its assets to a subsidiary of Continental Oil in 1963.
[2] American Car & Foundry changed its name to ACF Industries in 1954.
[3] American Cotton Oil merged into Best Foods (then known as Gold Dust Corp.) in 1924 and is now part of CPC International.
[4] American Locomotive changed its name to Alco Products in 1955, sold its assets and changed its name to Citadel Industries in 1964, and was liquidated by 1976.
[5] American Radiator & Standard Sanitary changed its name to American Standard in 1967.
[6] American Smelting & Refining changed its name to ASARCO in 1975.
[7] American Sugar Refining combined with Spreckels Sugar to form American Sugar Co. in 1963. The name was changed to Amstar in 1970.
[8] American Viscose sold its assets in 1963 and changed its name to A.V.C. Corp.
[9] American Woolen merged into Textron in 1955.
[10] Anaconda merged into Atlantic Richfield in 1977.
[11] Armour & Co. merged into Greyhound in 1970.
[12] Associated Oil merged with Tide Water Oil in 1926 to form Tide Water Associated Oil.
[13] Atlantic, Gulf & West Indies Steamship Lines was liquidated in 1951.

TABLE A-6 THE TOP 100 SURVIVORS, DROPOUTS, AND NEWCOMERS—(Continued)

Each of the 209 companies listed alphabetically below has appeared on one or more of the listings of the top 100 industrial companies in the United States. After each name appears the ranking it attained in each period in accordance with its asset size.

Company	1917	1929	1945	1966	1977
Baldwin Locomotive Works[14]	78	100	—	—	—
Beatrice Foods	—	—	—	—	83
Bendix Aviation[15]	—	—	44	—	—
Bethlehem Steel	3	5	7	19	28
Boeing	—	—	—	41	94
Borden	—	53	70	76	—
Burlington Industries	—	—	—	66	—
Burroughs	—	—	—	—	64
Calumet & Hecla Mining[16]	88	—	—	—	—
Cambria Steel[17]	22	—	—	—	—
Caterpillar Tractor	—	—	—	54	37
Celanese	—	—	86	34	95
Central Leather[18]	24	—	—	—	—
Chile Copper[19]	29	—	—	—	—

Chrysler	—	44	25	14	18
Cities Service[20]	—	—	—	31	43
Coca-Cola	—	—	74	—	96
Colorado Fuel & Iron[21]	55	—	—	—	—
Consolidation Coal[22]	27	—	—	—	—
Continental Can (Continental Group)	—	—	72	69	76
Continental Oil	—	48	73	23	23
Corn Products Refining (Corn Products Co.)[23]	41	76	—	97	—
Crane	95	84	—	—	—
Crown Zellerbach	—	82	—	79	—
Crucible Steel[24]	59	78	—	—	—
Cuba Cane Sugar[25]	63	99	—	—	—

[14] Baldwin Locomotive Works became Baldwin-Lima-Hamilton in 1950 and merged into Armour & Co. in 1965

[15] Bendix Aviation changed its name to Bendix Corp. in 1960.

[16] Calumet & Hecla Mining was acquired by Universal Oil Products (now UOP Inc.) in 1968.

[17] Cambria Steel was acquired by Bethlehem Steel in 1923.

[18] Central Leather became U.S. Leather and was liquidated in 1952.

[19] Chile Copper was acquired by Anaconda Copper in 1929.

[20] Cities Service was considered a utility holding company for periods prior to 1966.

[21] Colorado Fuel & Iron changed its name to CF & I Steel in 1966. It is now controlled by Crane Co.

[22] Consolidation Coal merged with Pittsburgh Coal to form Pittsburgh Consolidation Coal in 1945 (name changed to Consolidation Coal in 1958). Its assets were sold in 1966 and the company was liquidated by 1967.

[23] Corn Products Co. changed its name to CPC International in 1969.

[24] Crucible Steel merged into Colt Industries in 1968.

[25] Cuba Cane Sugar was reorganized as Cuba Cane Products in 1930 and Cuban Atlantic Sugar in 1935. It was liquidated by 1959.

TABLE A-6 THE TOP 100 SURVIVORS, DROPOUTS, AND NEWCOMERS—*(Continued)*

Each of the 209 companies listed alphabetically below has appeared on one or more of the listings of the top 100 industrial companies in the United States. After each name appears the ranking it attained in each period in accordance with its asset size.

Company	1917	1929	1945	1966	1977
Cudahy Packing[26]	84	—	—	—	—
Curtiss-Wright	—	—	28	—	—
Deere & Co.	79	—	63	50	52
Distillers Corp.-Seagrams (Seagram Co.)	—	—	66	78	80
Distillers Securities[27]	98	—	—	—	—
Douglas Aircraft[28]	—	—	82	84	—
Dow Chemical	—	—	99	33	20
E. I. du Pont de Nemours	7	12	5	16	19
Eastman Kodak	85	60	34	35	24
Engelhard Minerals & Chem.	—	—	—	—	99
Federated Department Stores	—	—	—	87	73
Firestone Tire & Rubber	—	62	35	42	50
FMC	—	—	—	98	93
Ford Motor	20	6	10	3	6
General Chemical[29]	90	—	—	—	—

General Dynamics	—	—	—	92	—
General Electric	10	11	8	9	11
General Foods	—	—	77	74	68
General Motors	30	3	3	2	2
General Telephone & Electronics[30]	—	—	—	11	8
General Theatres Equip.[31]	—	91	—	—	—
Georgia-Pacific	—	—	—	70	62
Getty Oil	—	—	—	—	41
Glen Alden Coal[32]	—	57	55	83	—
B. F. Goodrich	23	59	31	26	—
Goodyear Tire & Rubber	73	33	—	40	31
W. R. Grace	52	—	52	81	60
Great Atlantic & Pacific Tea	—	67	—	—	—
Great Northern Iron Ore	56	—	—	—	—

[26] Cudahy Packing changed its name to Cudahy Co. in 1966 and was merged into General Host in 1972.

[27] Distillers Securities became U.S. Food Products in 1919. It was reorganized as National Distillers Products in 1924. Name changed to National Distillers & Chemical in 1957.

[28] Douglas Aircraft merged into McDonnell Co. in 1967 to form McDonnell Douglas.

[29] General Chemical became part of Allied Chemical & Dye, which was formed in 1920.

[30] General Telephone & Electronics was considered a public utility for periods prior to 1966.

[31] General Theatres Equipment was reorganized in 1936 and changed its name to General Precision Equipment in 1942. Merged into Singer Co. in 1968.

[32] Glen Alden Coal changed its name to Glen Alden Corp. in 1955. Changed name to Rapid-American in 1972 after acquiring company of same name.

TABLE A-6 THE TOP 100 SURVIVORS, DROPOUTS, AND NEWCOMERS—(*Continued*)

Each of the 209 companies listed alphabetically below has appeared on one or more of the listings of the top 100 industrial companies in the United States. After each name appears the ranking it attained in each period in accordance with its asset size.

Company	1917	1929	1945	1966	1977
Greene Cananea Copper[33]	89	—	—	—	—
Gulf & Western Industries	—	—	—	—	48
Gulf Oil	49	15	12	5	9
Halliburton	—	—	—	—	63
Hearst Consolidated Publications[34]	—	—	88	—	—
Honeywell	—	—	—	88	74
Humble Oil & Refining[35]	—	36	15	—	—
IC Industries[36]	—	—	—	—	67
Inland Steel	91	97	67	62	86
International Business Machines	—	—	94	10	5
International Harvester	6	17	14	29	45
International Match[37]	—	42	—	—	—
International Mercantile Marine[38]	11	—	—	—	—
International Nickel (Inco Ltd.)	81	51	37	61	42
International Paper	71	25	45	47	40

International Shoe[39]	—	88	—	—	—
Int'l. Tel. & Tel.[40]	17	—	—	22	13
Jones & Laughlin Steel[41]	—	41	40	55	—
Kaiser Aluminum & Chem.	—	—	—	52	77
Kennecott Copper	25	19	18	57	72
Koppers	—	32	—	—	—
S. S. Kresge (K Mart)	—	90	75	—	54
Lackawanna Steel[42]	48	—	—	—	—
Lehigh Coal & Navigation	67	—	—	—	—
Libby, McNeill & Libby[43]	96	—	—	—	—
Liggett & Myers Tobacco[44]	45	66	38	—	—
Litton Industries	—	—	—	91	87
Lockheed Aircraft	—	—	78	93	—

[33] Greene Cananea Copper was acquired by Anaconda Copper in 1929.
[34] Hearst Consolidated Publications merged into Hearst Corp. in 1964.
[35] Humble Oil & Refining was acquired by Standard Oil (N.J.) in 1959.
[36] IC Industries was considered a railroad for prior periods.
[37] International Match was liquidated in 1932.
[38] International Mercantile Marine changed its name to U.S. Lines in 1943 and merged into Walter Kidde & Co. in 1969.
[39] International Shoe changed its name to Interco in 1966.
[40] International Telephone & Telegraph was considered a public utility for periods prior to 1966.
[41] Jones & Laughlin Steel merged into LTV Corp. in 1974.
[42] Lackawanna Steel was acquired by Bethlehem Steel in 1922.
[43] Libby, McNeill & Libby merged into Nestle Alimentana S.A. in 1976.
[44] Liggett & Myers Tobacco changed its name to Liggett Group in 1976.

TABLE A-6 THE TOP 100 SURVIVORS, DROPOUTS, AND NEWCOMERS—(*Continued*)

Each of the 209 companies listed alphabetically below has appeared on one or more of the listings of the top 100 industrial companies in the United States. After each name appears the ranking it attained in each period in accordance with its asset size.

Company	1917	1929	1945	1966	1977
Loew's Inc.[45]	—	79	58	—	—
Long Bell Lumber[46]	—	85	—	—	—
P. Lorillard[47]	86	94	—	—	—
LTV	—	—	—	—	81
Magnolia Petroleum[48]	37	—	—	—	—
Marshall Field	—	70	—	—	—
Glenn L. Martin[49]	—	—	91	—	—
May Department Stores	—	—	—	89	—
McDonnell Douglas	—	—	—	—	82
Mexican Petroleum[50]	64	—	—	—	—
Midvale Steel & Ordnance[51]	8	—	—	—	—
Minnesota Mining & Mfg.	—	—	—	71	49
Monsanto	—	—	—	28	35
Montgomery Ward[52]	—	50	27	32	—
Morris & Co.[53]	65	—	—	—	—

National Biscuit[54]	76	72	95	—	—
National Dairy Products (Kraft)	—	52	47	77	100
National Distillers Prod. (National Distillers & Chem.)	—	—	93	90	—
National Lead[55]	68	93	100	—	—
National Steel	—	80	43	53	58
NCR	—	—	—	—	71
Occidental Petroleum	—	—	—	—	36
Ohio Cities Gas (Pure Oil)[56]	42	43	56	80	—
Ojio Oil (Marathon Oil)	60	89	96	80	51
Olin Mathieson Chemical[57]	—	—	—	51	—
Owens-Illinois	—	—	—	82	75

[45] Loew's, Inc. changed its name to Metro-Goldwyn-Mayer in 1960.
[46] Long Bell Lumber merged into International Paper in 1956.
[47] P. Lorillard changed its name to Lorillard Corp. in 1968 and in the same year merged into Loew's Theatres (now Loew's Corp.)
[48] Magnolia Petroleum merged into Standard Oil (N.Y.) in 1925.
[49] Glenn L. Martin Co. changed its name to Martin Co. in 1957 and merged with American-Marietta in 1961 to form Martin-Marietta.
[50] Mexican Petroleum was acquired by Pan American Petroleum & Transport in 1919.
[51] Midvale Steel & Ordnance was acquired by Bethlehem Steel in 1923.
[52] Montgomery Ward merged with Container Corp. of America in 1968 to form Marcor. Marcor merged into Mobil Corp. in 1976.
[53] Morris & Co. was acquired by Armour & Co. in 1923.
[54] National Biscuit changed its name to Nabisco in 1971.
[55] National Lead changed its name to NL Industries in 1971.
[56] Ohio Cities Gas changed its name to Pure Oil in 1920 and merged into Union Oil of California in 1965.
[57] Olin Mathieson Chemical changed its name to Olin Corp. in 1969.

TABLE A-6 THE TOP 100 SURVIVORS, DROPOUTS, AND NEWCOMERS—(Continued)

Each of the 209 companies listed alphabetically below has appeared on one or more of the listings of the top 100 industrial companies in the United States. After each name appears the ranking it attained in each period in accordance with its asset size.

Company	1917	1929	1945	1966	1977
Pan American Petroleum & Transport[58]	99	—	—	—	—
Paramount Pictures[59]	—	37	76	—	—
J. C. Penney	—	—	65	85	47
Pfizer	—	—	—	—	79
Phelps Dodge	15	77	64	—	44
Philadelphia & Reading Coal & Iron[60]	—	74	97	—	—
Phillips Petroleum	—	68	32	18	27
Pittsburgh Coal[61]	39	54	—	—	—
Pittsburgh Plate Glass (PPG Industries)	—	98	83	73	88
Prairie Oil & Gas[62]	50	45	—	—	—
Prairie Pipe Line	—	69	—	—	—
Procter & Gamble	57	92	68	38	34
Pullman	26	21	41	—	—
Radio Corp. of America (RCA Corp.)	—	64	80	39	38
Republic Iron & Steel (Republic Steel)	43	20	26	44	70

Reynolds Metals	—	—	—	46	69
R. J. Reynolds Tobacco (R. J. Reynolds Inds.)	82	61	33	49	32
Richfield Oil[63]	—	73	—	—	53
Rockwell International	—	—	—	—	53
St. Regis Paper	—	—	—	94	—
Schenley Distillers[64]	—	—	69	—	—
Schlumberger	—	—	—	—	90
Sears, Roebuck	32	30	16	7	10
Shell Union Oil (Shell Oil)	—	13	22	15	16
Signal Companies	—	—	—	—	98
Sinclair Consolidated Oil (Sinclair Oil)[65]	—	16	20	30	—
Sinclair Crude Oil Purchasing Co.[66]	—	87	—	—	—

[58] Pan American Petroleum & Transport merged into Standard Oil (Ind.) in 1954.

[59] Paramount Pictures merged into Gulf & Western Industries in 1966.

[60] Philadelphia & Reading Coal & Iron changed its name to Philadelphia & Reading Corp. in 1955. It is now controlled by Northwest Industries.

[61] Pittsburgh Coal merged with Consolidation Coal to form Pittsburgh Consolidation Coal in 1945 (name changed to Consolidation Coal in 1958). Its assets were sold in 1966, and the company was liquidated in 1967.

[62] Prairie Oil & Gas and Prairie Pipe Line merged into Consolidated Oil in 1932. Consolidated subsequently changed its name to Sinclair Oil (1943) and merged into Atlantic Richfield (1969).

[63] Richfield Oil merged into Atlantic Refining (now Atlantic Richfield) in 1966.

[64] Schenley Distillers changed its name to Schenley Industries in 1948. It merged into Glen Alden Corp. (now Rapid-American) in 1971.

[65] Sinclair Consolidated Oil changed its name to Sinclair Oil in 1943 and merged into Atlantic Richfield in 1969.

[66] Sinclair Crude Oil Purchasing Co. was dissolved in 1939.

TABLE A-6 THE TOP 100 SURVIVORS, DROPOUTS, AND NEWCOMERS—*(Continued)*

Each of the 209 companies listed alphabetically below has appeared on one or more of the listings of the top 100 industrial companies in the United States. After each name appears the ranking it attained in each period in accordance with its asset size.

Company	1917	1929	1945	1966	1977
Sinclair Gulf[67]	97	—	—	—	—
Sinclair Oil & Rfg.	69	—	—	—	—
Singer Manufacturing (Singer Co.)	16	27	54	67	—
Socony Vacuum Oil (Mobil Corp.)	—	—	4	8	3
Sperry Rand	—	—	—	60	55
Standard Oil (Calif.)	35	10	11	12	7
Standard Oil (Ind.)	36	4	6	13	12
Standard Oil (N.J.) (Exxon)	2	2	1	1	1
Standard Oil (N.Y.)[68]	14	7	—	—	—
Standard Oil (Ohio)	—	—	89	—	22
Studebaker[69]	80	71	—	—	—
Sun Oil (Sun Co.)	—	—	61	43	29
Sunray DX Oil[70]	—	—	—	100	—
Swift & Co.[71]	5	18	29	95	—
Tenneco[72]	—	—	—	17	17

Texas Co. (Texaco)	33	9	9	4	4
Tide Water Associated Oil Tidewater Oil[73]	—	31	50	64	—
TRW	—	—	—	—	97
Twentieth Century-Fox Film	—	—	85	—	—
Union Carbide & Carbon (Union Carbide Corp.)	21	24	23	21	21
Union Oil of California	74	35	53	27	33
United Aircraft (United Technologies)	—	—	71	58	61
United Cigar Stores of America[74]	—	63	—	—	—
United Drug[75]	—	83	—	—	—
United Fruit[76]	44	40	49	—	—
United Motors[77]	92	—	—	—	—

[67] Sinclair Gulf and Sinclair Oil & Refining formed Sinclair Consolidated Oil in 1919.

[68] Standard Oil (N.Y.) combined with Vacuum Oil in 1931 to form Socony Vacuum Oil.

[69] Studebaker sold its assets in 1954 to Packard Motor Car, which changed its name to Studebaker-Packard. Studebaker-Packard became part of Studebaker-Worthington in 1967.

[70] Sunray DX Oil merged into Sun Oil in 1968.

[71] Swift & Co. changed its name to Esmark in 1973.

[72] Tenneco, formerly Tennessee Gas Transmission, was considered a public utility for periods prior to 1966.

[73] Tidewater Oil merged into Getty Oil in 1967.

[74] United Cigar Stores of America was reorganized in 1937 to become United Cigar-Whelan Stores. It changed its name to Cadence Industries in 1970.

[75] United Drug was consolidated with Sterling Products in 1928 to form Drug Inc. which in 1933 was broken up into five units, including United Drug. United has been known as Dart Industries since 1969.

[76] United Fruit changed its name to United Brands in 1970.

[77] United Motors dissolved in 1919 after selling its assets to General Motors.

TABLE A-6 THE TOP 100 SURVIVORS, DROPOUTS, AND NEWCOMERS—*(Continued)*

Each of the 209 companies listed alphabetically below has appeared on one or more of the listings of the top 100 industrial companies in the United States. After each name appears the ranking it attained in each period in accordance with its asset size.

Company	1917	1929	1945	1966	1977
United Shoe Machinery[78]	77	—	98	—	—
U.S. Plywood (Champion International)	—	—	—	86	78
U.S. Rubber (Uniroyal)	9	23	46	63	—
U.S. Smelting, Refining & Mining[79]	72	1	—	—	14
U.S. Steel	1	—	2	6	—
United Verde Extension Mining[80]	100	—	—	—	—
Utah Copper[81]	70	—	—	—	—
Vacuum Oil[82]	75	46	—	—	—
Virginia Carolina Chem.[83]	46	—	—	—	—
Warner Brothers Pictures[84]	—	56	62	—	—
Warner-Lambert	—	—	—	—	92
Western Electric[85]	54	22	19	20	26
Westinghouse Electric & Mfg. (Westinghouse Electric Corp.)	18	29	21	25	25

Weyerhaeuser Timber (Weyerhaeuser Co.)	—	—	79	65	39
Wheeling Steel[86]	—	75	92	—	—
Willys-Overland[87]	40	—	—	—	—
Wilson & Co.[88]	51	58	—	—	—
F. W. Woolworth	62	—	36	68	85
Xerox	—	—	—	—	30
Youngstown Sheet & Tube[89]	53	38	48	72	—

[78] United Shoe Machinery changed its name to USM Corp. in 1968 and merged into Emhart in 1976.
[79] United States Smelting Refining & Mining changed its name to UV Industries in 1972.
[80] United Verde Extension Mining was liquidated in 1937.
[81] Utah Copper merged into Kennecott Copper in 1936.
[82] Vacuum Oil combined with Standard Oil (N.Y.) in 1931 to form Socony Vacuum Oil.
[83] Virginia Carolina Chemical merged into Socony Mobil Oil (now Mobil Corp.) in 1963.
[84] Warner Brothers Pictures merged into Seven Arts Productions in 1967, forming Warner Bros.-Seven Arts Ltd. (presently part of Warner Communications).
[85] Western Electric is wholly owned by AT&T.
[86] Wheeling Steel changed its name to Wheeling-Pittsburgh Steel in 1968.
[87] Willys-Overland Co. reorganized in 1936, became Overland Corp., and was liquidated.
[88] Wilson & Co. merged into Ling-Temco-Vought (now LTV Corp.) in 1967.
[89] Youngstown Sheet & Tube merged with Lykes Corp. in 1969 to form Lykes-Youngstown, which changed its name to Lykes Corp. in 1976.

GLOSSARY[1]

Accrued Interest Interest accrued on a bond since the last interest payment was made. The buyer of the bonds pays the market price plus accrued interest. Exceptions include bonds that are in default and income bonds.

Annual Report The formal financial statement issued yearly by a corporation. The annual report shows assets, liabilities, earnings—how the company stood at the close of the business year, how it fared profit-wise during the year, and other information of interest to shareowners.

[1] © New York Stock Exchange, Inc., 1978. Reprinted by permission.

Assets   Everything a corporation owns or due to it: cash, investments, money due to it, materials, and inventories, which are called *current assets*; buildings and machinery, which are known as *fixed assets*; and patents and goodwill called *intangible assets*.

Balance Sheet   A condensed financial statement showing the nature and amount of a company's assets, liabilities, and capital on a given date. In dollar amounts the balance sheet shows what the company owned, what it owed, and the ownership interest in the company of its stockholders.

Bearer Bond   A bond which does not have the owner's name registered on the books of the issuer and which is payable to the holder.

Bid and Asked   Often referred to as a *quotation* or *quote*. The *bid* is the highest price anyone has declared that he wants to pay for a security at a given time; the *asked* is the lowest price anyone will take at the same time.

Bond   Basically an IOU or promissory note of a corporation, usually issued in multiples of $1000 or $5000, although $100 and $500 denominations are not unknown. A bond is evidence of a debt on which the issuing company usually promises to pay the bondholders a specified amount of interest for a specified length of time, and to repay the loan on the expiration date. In every case a bond represents debt—its holder is a creditor of the corporation and not a part owner, as is the shareholder. In most cases, bonds are secured by a mortgage.

Book Value   An accounting term. Book value of a stock is determined from a company's records, by adding all assets then deducting all debts and other liabilities, plus the liquidation price of any preferred issues. The sum arrived at is divided by the number of common shares outstanding, and the result is book value per common share. Book value of the assets of a company or a security may have little or no significant relationship to market value.

Broker   An agent who handles the public's orders to buy and sell securities, commodities, or other property. For this service a commission is charged.

Callable   A bond issue, all or part of which may be redeemed by the issuing corporation under definite conditions before maturity. The term also applies to preferred shares which may be redeemed by the issuing corporation.

Capital Stock   All shares representing ownership of a business, including preferred and common.

Capitalization   Total amount of the various securities issued by a corporation. Capitalization may include bonds, debentures, preferred and common stock, and surplus. Bonds and debentures are usually carried on the books of the issuing company in terms of their par or face value. Preferred and common shares may be carried in terms of par or stated value. Stated value may be an arbitrary figure decided upon by the directors or may represent the amount received by the company from the sale of the securities at the time of issuance.

Certificate   The actual piece of paper which is evidence of ownership of stock in a corporation. Watermarked paper is finely engraved with delicate etchings to discourage forgery. Loss of a certificate may at the least cause a great deal of inconvenience—at the worst, financial loss.

Collateral Trust Bond   A bond secured by collateral deposited with a trustee. The collateral is often the stocks or bonds of companies controlled by the issuing company, but it may be other securities.

Common Stock   Securities which represent an ownership interest in a corporation. If the company has also issued preferred stock, both common and preferred have ownership rights. The preferred normally is limited to a fixed dividend but has prior claim on dividends and, in the event of liquidation, assets. Claims of both common and preferred stockholders are junior to claims of bondholders or other creditors of the company. Common stockholders assume the greater risk, but generally they exercise the greater control and may gain the greater reward in the form of dividends and capital appreciation. The terms "common stock" and "capital stock" are often used interchangeably when the company has no preferred stock.

Convertible   A bond, debenture, or preferred share which may be exchanged by the owner for common stock or another security, usually of the same company, in accordance with the terms of the issue.

Coupon Bond   Bond with interest coupons attached. The coupons are clipped as they come due and are presented by the holder for payment of interest.

Cumulative Preferred   A stock having a provision that if one or more dividends are omitted, the omitted dividends must be paid before dividends may be paid on the company's common stock.

Dealer   An individual or firm in the securities business acting as a principal rather than as an agent. Typically, a dealer buys for his own account and sells to a customer from his own inventory. The dealer's profit or loss is the difference between the price he pays and the price he receives for the same security. The dealer's confirmation must disclose to his customer that he has acted as principal. The same individual or firm may function, at different times, either as broker or dealer.

Debenture   A promissory note backed by the general credit of a company and usually not secured by a mortgage or lien on any specific property.

Depreciation   Normally, charges against earnings to write off the cost, less salvage value, of an asset over its estimated useful life. It is a bookkeeping entry and does not represent any cash outlay, nor are any funds earmarked for the purpose.

Dividend   The payment designated by the Board of Directors to be distributed pro rata among the shares outstanding. On preferred shares, it is generally a fixed amount. On common shares, the dividend varies with the fortunes of the company and the amount of cash on hand, and may be omitted if business is poor or the directors determine to withhold earnings to invest in plant and equipment. Sometimes a company will pay a dividend out of past earnings even if it is not currently operating at a profit.

Earnings Report A statement—also called an income statement—issued by a company showing its earnings or losses over a given period. The earnings report lists the income earned, expenses, and the net result.

Equipment Trust Certificate A type of security, generally issued by a railroad, to pay for new equipment. Title to the equipment, such as a locomotive, is held by a trustee until the notes are paid off. An equipment trust certificate is usually secured by a first claim on the equipment.

Equity The ownership interest of common and preferred stockholders in a company. Also refers to excess of value of securities over the debit balance in a margin account.

Face Value The value of a bond that appears on the face of the bond, unless the value is otherwise specified by the issuing company. Face value is ordinarily the amount the issuing company promises to pay at maturity. Face value is not an indication of market value. Sometimes referred to as *par value*.

Flat Income Bond This term means that the price at which a bond is traded includes consideration for all unpaid accruals of interest. Bonds which are in default of interest or principal are traded flat. Income bonds, which pay interest only to the extent earned, are usually traded flat. All other bonds are usually dealt in "and interest," which means that the buyer pays to the seller the market price plus interest accrued since the last payment date.

General Mortgage Bond A bond which is secured by a blanket mortgate on the company's property, but which may be outranked by one or more other mortgages.

Government Bonds   Obligations of the U.S. government, regarded as the highest-grade issues in existence.

Guaranteed Bond   A bond which has interest or principal, or both, guaranteed by a company other than the issuer. Usually found in the railroad industry when large roads, leasing sections of trackage owned by small railroads, may guarantee the bonds of the smaller road.

Guaranteed Stock   Usually preferred stock on which dividends are guaranteed by another company, under much the same circumstances as when a bond is guaranteed.

Income Bond   Generally income bonds promise to repay principal but to pay interest only when earned. In some cases unpaid interest on an income bond may accumulate as a claim against the corporation when the bond becomes due. An income bond may also be issued in lieu of preferred stock.

Indenture   A written agreement under which bonds and debentures are issued, setting forth maturity date, interest rate, and other terms.

Interest   Payments a borrower pays a lender for the use of his money. A corporation pays interest on its bonds to its bondholders.

Issue   Any of a company's securities, or the act of distributing such securities.

Liabilities   All the claims against a corporation. Liabilities include accounts and wages and salaries payable, dividends declared payable, accrued taxes payable, and fixed or long-term liabilities such as mortgage bonds, debentures, and bank loans.

Lien   A claim against property. A bond is usually secured by a lien against specified property of a company.

Liquidation   The process of converting securities or other property into cash; the dissolution of a company, with cash remaining after sale of its assets and payment of all indebtedness being distributed to the shareholders.

Maturity The date on which a loan or a bond or debenture comes due and is to be paid off.

Mortgage Bond A bond secured by a mortgage on a property. The value of the property may or may not equal the value of the so-called mortgage bonds issued against it.

Municipal Bond A bond issued by a state or a political subdivision, such as county, city, town, or village. The term also designates bonds issued by state agencies and authorities. In general, interest paid on municipal bonds is exempt from federal income taxes and state and local income taxes within the state of issue.

NASD The National Association of Securities Dealers, Inc., an association of brokers and dealers in the over-the-counter securities business. The Association has the power to expel members who have been declared guilty of unethical practices. NASD is dedicated to—among other objectives— "adopt, administer and enforce rules of fair practice and rules to prevent fraudulent and manipulative acts and practices, and in general to promote just and equitable principles of trade for the protection of investors."

New Issue A stock or bond sold by a corporation for the first time. Proceeds may be issued to retire outstanding securities of the company, for new plant or equipment, or for additional working capital.

Noncumulative A preferred stock on which unpaid dividends do not accrue. Omitted dividends are, as a rule, gone forever.

Offer The price at which a person is ready to sell. Opposed to bid, the price at which one is ready to buy.

Par In the case of a common share, par means a dollar amount assigned to the share by the company's charter. Par value may also be used to compute the dollar amount of the common shares on the balance sheet. Par value has little significance so far as market value of common stock is concerned. Many companies today issue no-par stock but give a stated per share value on the balance sheet. Int the case of preferred shares and bonds, however, par is important. It often signifies the dollar value upon which dividends on preferred stocks, and interest on bonds, are figured. The issuer of a 6 percent bond promises to pay that percentage of the bond's par value annually.

Participating Preferred   A preferred stock which is entitled to its stated dividend and, also, to additional dividends on a specified basis upon payment of dividends on the common stock.

Preferred Stock   A class of stock with a claim on the company's earnings before payment may be made on the common stock and usually entitled to priority over common stock if the company liquidates. Usually entitled to dividends at a specified rate—when declared by the Board of Directors and before payment of a dividend on the common stock—depending upon the terms of the issue.

Premium   The amount by which a preferred stock, bond, or option may sell above its par value. In the case of a new issue of bonds or stocks, premium is the amount the market price rises over the original selling price. Also refers to a charge sometimes made when a stock is borrowed to make delivery on a short sale. May also refer to redemption price of a bond or preferred stock if it is higher than face value.

Refinancing   Same as refunding. New securities are sold by a company, and the money is used to retire existing securities. Object may be to save interest costs, extend the maturity of the loan, or both.

Registered Bond   A bond which is registered on the books of the issuing company in the name of the owner. It can be transferred only when endorsed by the registered owner.

Registrar   Usually a trust company or bank charged with the responsibility of preventing the issuance of more stock than authorized by a company.

Serial Bond   An issue which matures in part at periodic stated intervals.

Sinking Fund   Money regularly set aside by a company to redeem its bonds, debentures, or preferred stock from time to time as specified in the indenture or charter.

Split   The division of the outstanding shares of a corporation into a larger number of shares. A 3-for-1 split by a company with 1 million shares outstanding results in 3 million shares outstanding. Each holder of 100 shares before the 3-for-1 split would have 300 shares, although his proportionate equity in the company would remain the same; 100 parts of 1 million are the equivalent of 300 parts of 3 million. Ordinarily splits must be voted by directors and approved by shareholders.

Stock Dividend   A dividend paid in securities rather than cash. The dividend may be additional shares of the issuing company, or shares of another company (usually a subsidiary) held by the company.

Stockholder of Record   A stockholder whose name is registered on the books of the issuing corporation.

Street Name   Securities held in the name of a broker instead of his customer's name are said to be carried in a "street name." This occurs when the securities have been bought on margin or when the customer wishes the security to be held by the broker.

Transfer   This term may refer to two different operations. One is the delivery of a stock certificate from the seller's broker to the buyer's broker and legal change of ownership, normally accomplished within a few days; the other is the recording of the change of ownership on the books of the corporation by the transfer agent. When the purchaser's name is recorded on the books of the company, dividends, notices of meetings, proxies, financial reports, and all pertinent literature sent by the issuer to its securities holders are mailed direct to the new owner.

Transfer Agent   A transfer agent keeps a record of the name of each registered shareowner, his or her address, and the number of shares owned, and sees that certificates presented to his office for transfer are properly canceled and new certificates issued in the name of the transferee.

Treasury Stock   Stock issued by a company but later reacquired. It may be held in the company's treasury indefinitely, reissued to the public, or retired. Treasury stock receives no dividends and has no vote while held by the company.

Voting Right   The stockholder's right to vote his stock in the affairs of his company. Most common shares have one vote each. Preferred stock usually has the right to vote when preferred dividends are in default for a specified period. The right to vote may be delegated by the stockholder to another person.

Note: The authors would be grateful for any information regarding readers' investigations into their own questioned stocks. In particular, we would be very happy to hear of any successful finds for possible future publication. Please address your letters to Mr. Rocco Carlucci, 208 Hawthorne Avenue, Staten Island, NY 10314.

INDEX

Acquisitions:
  effects of, on stock, 9–11
  1948–1958, 14
Addresses:
  of Arnold Bernhard & Co.,
    Inc., 92
  of corporate officials, 60–62
  of corporations, 60, 70, 71
  of Financial Information, Inc.,
    66n.
  of Investment Statistics
    Laboratory, 91

Addresses (Cont.):
  mailing, Section of Public
    Reference (SEC), 53
  of Moody's Investors Service,
    Inc., 91
  of National Association of
    Securities Dealers, 59
  of National Quotation Bureau
    Incorporated, 69n.
  of offices of (states) secretaries
    of state, 44–50
  of R. M. Smythe & Co., Inc., 64n.

187

Addresses (*Cont.*):
  of search companies, 22*n*., 25*n*.
  of Securities and Exchange
    Commission regional and
    branch offices, 54–55
  of Standard & Poor's
    Corporation, 79*n*.
  of Wiesenberger Financial
    Services, 92
American Bank Note Company,
  110–113
American Investor (magazine), 77
Anderson, 10
Annual reports, 61
Arnold Bernhard & Co., Inc., 92
Articles of incorporation, 41
Asked price, defined, 75
Autographs, as collectors' items,
  98, 99

Bank and Quotation Record
  (magazine), 77
*Barron's: National Business and
  Financial Weekly*
  (newspaper), 77
Bid prices, defined, 75
Bonds, 69
Branch offices, Securities and
  Exchange Commission, 55
Broker/dealers, National
  Association of Securities
  Dealers and, 58–59
Bureau of Economics (of FTC),
  12, 14
Burr, Aaron, 99
Business Week (magazine), 77

Cameo printing (letterpress), 108

Canadian provinces, contacting
  officials in, for information,
  49–50
Caribbean officials, contacting, 50
Carnegie, Andrew, 99
Central American officials,
  contacting, 50
Charters (*see* Corporate charters)
Color reproduction, identifying
  counterfeit documents made
  by, table, 114–116
Color xerography, 110, 111
*Commercial and Financial
  Chronicle* (newspaper), 77
Common stock, corporate,
  example, 70, 72–73
Competition, corporate, 120–123
Conglomerates, 14
  defined, 13
Consolidations, defined, 13
Corporate charters:
  cancellation of, 42
  information from, 41
Corporation Records (Standard &
  Poor's), 90
Corporation Register (Standard &
  Poor's), 61
Corporations:
  competition among, 120–123
  direct contact with, 60–62
  existing, as source of
    information, 40
  full legal name and exact
    spelling of names of, 34
  top 100 industrial, tables (1917–
    1977), 124–159
  top 100 survivors, dropouts, and
    newcomers, table (1917–
    1977), 160–175
  (*See also* Corporate charters;
    Incorporation)

Counterfeit documents, 103–117
  aids in detecting, 111–113
  copying difficulty as deterrent
    to producing, 105–106
  identifying, table, 114–116
  quick checks for, 117
Counterstock, use of term, 5

Dates:
  of incorporation, 37
  of issue of stock, 38
  record, 74
Debentures, 69
Detection (see Counterfeit
    documents)
Dilution, defined, 73
Directors, contacting, for
    information, 60, 61
Directory of Obsolete Securities
    (National Quotation Bureau),
    66–69
Disclosure, 51–52
Dividend Record (Standard &
    Poor's), 90
Dividends, corporate, example,
    70, 73–74
Drake, Edwin, 30
Dropouts:
  corporate, table (1917–1977),
    160–175
  (See also Corporations)

Earnings Forecaster (Standard &
    Poor's), 90
Ellis, Dwight H., Jr., 22
Elofsson, Peter, 4
Evans, Thomas M., 10
Exchange, The (magazine), 77

Fillmore, Millard, 98
Finance (magazine), 77
Financial Analyst's Journal, The
    (magazine), 77
Financial Information, Inc., 40,
    66
Financial Times (newspaper), 78
Financial World (magazine), 78
Fisher, Robert, Jr., 95n.
Fisher Manuals of Valuable and
    Worthless Securities (Robert
    D. Fisher), 97
Float, defined, 72
Forbes (magazine), 78, 119
Fortune (magazine), 78
Fraudulent securities, detection
    and recognition of (see
    Counterfeit documents)
Fundscope (magazine), 78

Galbraith, John Kenneth, 120
Glossary, 177–186
Goldfader, Ed, 10, 21n., 26, 28n.

Hamilton, Alexander, 7, 99
Herzog, Diana, 95n.
Herzog, John, 95n., 96–98, 100,
    101
Horizontal mergers, defined, 13
Hurley, Roy T., 122–123

Identification, counterfeit (see
    Counterfeit documents)
Identifying numbers of stock
    certificates, 37
Incorporation:
  articles of, 41

Incorporation (*Cont.*):
  offices of secretaries of states
    and, 41
  state of, example, 70, 71
  state and date of, 37
Industrials (*see* Corporations)
Industry Surveys (Standard &
    Poor's), 90
Intaglio printing, 108–112
  latent image in, 111–112
Investigation procedure,
    illustrated, 35
Investment Companies
    (Wiesenberger Financial
    Services), 92
Investment Dealers' Digest
    (magazine), 78
Investment Statistics Laboratory
    (ISL), 91
*ISL Daily Stock Price Index:
    American Stock Exchange*, 91
*ISL Daily Stock Price Index:
    New York Stock Exchange*, 91
*ISL Daily Stock Price Index:
    Over-the-Counter and
    Regional Exchanges*, 91
Issue, date of stock, 38

Journal of Commerce
    (newspaper), 78

Kircher, Donald, 123

Latent image, 111–112
Letterpress (cameo printing), 108

Letters:
  to company, sample,
    illustrated, 61
  to National Association of
    Securities Dealers, 59
  to Secretary of State,
    illustrated, 43
  to Securities and Exchange
    Commission, illustrated, 57
Lithography, 108, 110, 111
  identifying counterfeit
    documents made by, table,
    114–116
Little, Royal, 121
Livermore, James, 99

McClellan, George, 98–99
Magazines, 77–78
Map of Securities and Exchange
    Commission headquarters
    and its regional and branch
    offices, illustrated, 56
*Marvyn Scudder Manual of
    Extinct or Obsolete
    Companies* (R. M. Smythe),
    64
Massé, Micheline, 21*n.*, 22–25,
    27*n.*
Mattel, 100
Media General Financial Weekly
    (newspaper), 78
Mellon, Andrew, 99
Mergers:
  effects of, on stock, 9–11
  per year, in North America, 23
  trends in, 12–13
Mining securities, 95–101
Money (magazine), 78

Moody's Investors Service, Inc.,
91–92
*Moody's Manuals of Investment,
American and Foreign,* 92
Morgan, J. P., 99

Names:
corporate change in, example,
70–72
of legal owners of stock, 37–38
of officers and their titles, 38–
39
official corporate, 34, 70, 71
publication listing, example, 85
National Association of Securities
Dealers (NASD):
address for inquiries made of,
59
information from, 58–59
National Association of Securities
Dealers Automatic Quotation
System (NASDAQ), 75
National Bond Summary
(National Quotation Bureau),
70
National Daily Services (National
Quotation Bureau), 69
National Monthly Stock
Summary (National
Quotation Bureau), 41, 60,
69–70
example of information from,
70–76
National Quotation Bureau
Incorporated, 69
New York Stock and Exchange
Board, 8
New York Stock Exchange
(NYSE), 7–9, 109–110

Newcomers:
corporate, table (1917–1977),
160–175
(*See also* Corporations)
News media, information from,
41, 76–79
Newspapers, 77–79
Number:
identifying, of stock certificates,
37
of shares owned, 37

*Obscure American Securities and
Corporations* (R. M. Smythe),
97
Officers:
names and titles of corporate,
38–39
as source of information, 40,
60, 61
*Official Summary of Security
Transactions and Holdings*
(magazine), 78
Officials:
addresses of corporate, 60–62
of Canadian provinces, 49–50
Caribbean, 50
Central American, 50
Securities and Exchange
Commission, 53–55
(*See also* Officers; Secretary of
State, Office of)
O-T-C Market Chronicle
(newspaper), 78

Par value, 39–40
publication listing, example, 70,
72, 86
Periodicals, 77–79

"Pink Sheets" (National Daily
    Quotation Service), 69, 76
Planchettes, uses of, 110,
    112–113, 115
Printing (see Cameo printing;
    Intaglio printing;
    Lithography)
Public library, as information
    source, 63–92
Public offerings, corporate,
    example, 70, 74–75
Public Reference Room (SEC),
    53
Publications, 64–93

Questioned stock:
    creation of, 9
    estimated value of, 2
    examples showing positive side
        of, 15–19
    periods producing, 23–24

Recognition of counterfeit
    documents (see Counterfeit
    documents)
Record date, defined, 74
Regional offices of Securities and
    Exchange Commission,
    54–55
Registrars:
    as source of information, 40
    stock certificate and, 39
    Stock Transfer Department of,
        information from, 57–58
Registration statements, 52
Revere, Paul, 98
R. M. Smythe & Company,
    95–97
    as source of information, 40,
        64–66

Robert D. Fisher Manual of
    Valuable and Worthless
    Securities (R. M. Smythe),
    64–66
Robert D. Fisher Service, 97
Rockefeller, John D., 99

Sage, Henry, 99
Schwarzschild, O. P., 2
Search companies, addresses of,
    22n., 25n.
Secretary of State, Office of
    (states):
    addresses of, 44–50
    company addresses obtained
        through, 60
    contacting, 42–43
    letter to, illustrated, 43
    as source of information,
        40–43
Section of Public Reference,
    Office of Records and
    Service (SEC), 53
Securities and Exchange
    Commission (SEC), 2
    corporate literature from, 62
    letter for contacting,
        illustrated, 57
    as source of information, 40,
        51–57
Security Dealers of North
    America (Standard & Poor's),
    91
Security printing, 106–109
Shakespeare, William, 9
Signatures, as collectors' items,
    98, 99
Smythe, Roland M., 27, 97
Smythe, R. M., & Company,
    95–97

Spread, defined, 75
Standard & Poor's Corporation, 61, 79
Standard & Poor's Stock Guide, 79
definitions of abbreviations in, 85-91
illustrated, 80-84
Stated value, 39-40
States:
of incorporation, 37
(*See also* Secretary of State, Office of)
Statistical Bulletin (magazine), 78
Stock, origin of word, 5
Stock certificates:
as collectors' items, 97-101
data to be gathered from, 34-40
history of, 3-9
old, as counterfeit, 104
printing, 106-109
requirements for printing, 109-110
as starting point for investigation, 34
(*See also* Counterfeit documents)
Stock Market Information Service, Inc., 22n.
Stock Reports (Standard & Poor's), 61, 91
Stock trading, history of, 3-9
Surface printing, 108, 110
Suspension of trading, 51

Tally, use of word, 5
10-K (form) Statement, 61
Titles:
names and, of officers of corporation, 38-39
(*See also* Names)

Tracers Company of America, Inc., 25-26, 28-29
address of, 25n.
Trade, use of term, 5-6
Trading:
history of stock, 3-9
publication showing example of, 70, 75-76, 86-87
suspension of, 51
Transfer agents:
example of corporate, 70, 72
as source of information, 40, 57-58
stock certificates and, 39
Stock Transfer Department of, information from, 57-58

Value:
par and stated, 39-40
publication listing, example, 70, 72, 86
Value Line Investment Survey, The (Arnold Bernhard), 92
Vanderbilt, Cornelius, 99
Vertical mergers, defined, 13

Wall Street, forming of, as securities market, 6-9
Wall Street Journal (newspaper), 79
Wall Street Transcript (newspaper), 79
Wiesenberger Financial Services, 92
William IV (king of England), 5

"Yellow Sheets" (National Daily Quotation Service), 69